FARMHOUSE COOKBOOK

Sally Ashworth
Caroline Ellwood

TREASURE PRESS

First published by Octopus Books Ltd as the ''In the Kitchen'' section
of *Encyclopedia of Vegetable Gardening*.

This edition published by Treasure Press
59 Grosvenor Street
London W1

© 1977 Octopus Books Ltd

ISBN 0 907407 62 5

Printed in Hong Kong

Contents

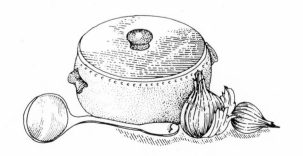

Soups & Hors-d'Oeuvre

Tomato Concertinas

Metric	Imperial
4 large tomatoes	4 large tomatoes
10–12 fresh basil leaves, chopped	10–12 fresh basil leaves, chopped
4 hard-boiled eggs, sliced	4 hard-boiled eggs, sliced
4 × 15ml spoons mayonnaise	4tbsps mayonnaise
2 spring onions or small piece onion, chopped	2 spring onions or small piece onion, chopped
Salt and pepper	Salt and pepper
16 strips green pepper	16 strips green pepper
½ cucumber, thinly sliced	½ cucumber, thinly sliced
Chervil sprigs	Chervil sprigs

This is a simple but unusual first course.
Put the tomatoes on small plates with the stalk ends down. Cut through centre almost to the base and make two similar cuts at each side of this first one. Put a little of the basil in each cut. Chill tomatoes. Just before serving put a slice of egg in each cut. Chop up rest of eggs and add to the mayonnaise with onions and seasoning. Put a line of this over the top of each tomato and decorate with the pepper strips. Surround each tomato with cucumber slices and chervil sprigs.
Serves 4

Potted Mushrooms*

Metric	Imperial
75g butter	3oz butter
½kg mushrooms, chopped	1lb mushrooms, chopped
1 × 5ml spoon dried thyme	1tsp dried thyme
Salt and freshly ground black pepper	Salt and freshly ground black pepper

A very old recipe, this is well worth reviving.
Melt 25g (1oz) of the butter in a saucepan, add the mushrooms, thyme and seasoning, and cook very slowly, covered, for 10 minutes. Using a slotted spoon, lift out the mushrooms and chop as finely as possible. Meanwhile, reduce the liquid in the pan by boiling without a lid until only 2–3 × 15ml spoons (2–3tbsps) remain. Mix in the mushrooms and check for seasoning. Pack tightly into 4 small (ramekin) dishes and smooth the top. When the mushrooms are cold, melt remaining butter, skim the surface and pour into each dish to cover the mushrooms completely. When set, cover with cling film, store in the refrigerator and eat within 4 days.
To freeze Wrap in cling film and then in freezer foil. Use within 3 months.
To thaw Thaw in the refrigerator for 3–4 hours.
Serves 4

Crispy Fried Vegetables with Garlic Mayonnaise

Metric	Imperial
½kg vegetables, see below	1lb vegetables, see below
Batter:	*Batter:*
2 eggs, separated	2 eggs, separated
300ml pale ale	½ pint pale ale
25g butter, melted	1oz butter, melted
175g flour	6oz flour
Salt and pepper	Salt and pepper
1 × 5ml spoon dry mustard	1tsp dry mustard
Garlic mayonnaise:	*Garlic mayonnaise:*
150ml mayonnaise	¼ pint mayonnaise
2 × 15ml spoons double cream	2tbsps double cream
2 cloves garlic, crushed	2 cloves garlic, crushed
1 × 15ml spoon dried mixed herbs	1tbsp dried mixed herbs
Salt and pepper	Salt and pepper

Try this unusual starter for a formal meal.
A variety of vegetables can be used for this recipe, including aubergine, celeriac, courgettes, cauliflower florets, Jerusalem artichokes, fennel, mushrooms, parsnip, etc. Courgettes and mushrooms are used raw; the others are steamed or boiled until half cooked. Cut into pieces the size of medium mushrooms.

To make the batter, mix egg yolks and ale together, add butter and beat until smooth. Gradually beat in the flour and seasoning. Whisk egg whites until very stiff, then fold into the batter.

Mix all the ingredients together for the mayonnaise and spoon into a serving dish.

Dip each piece of vegetable into the batter, making sure it is completely coated, and fry in hot deep fat at 180–190°C/350–375°F until golden brown and crisp. Drain on absorbent paper and serve at once with the mayonnaise.
Serves 4–6

* indicates suitability for freezing

Crispy fried vegetables and potted mushrooms

German Vegetable Soup*

Metric	Imperial
40g butter	1½oz butter
1 small onion, chopped	1 small onion, chopped
4 large carrots, peeled and thinly sliced	4 large carrots, peeled and thinly sliced
½ turnip or swede, peeled and diced	½ turnip or swede, peeled and diced
2–3 stalks celery, sliced	2–3 stalks celery, sliced
2 potatoes, peeled and diced	2 potatoes, peeled and diced
1 medium leek, sliced	1 medium leek, sliced
1 litre beef stock	2 pints beef stock
Salt and pepper	Salt and pepper
6 × 15ml spoons peas, fresh or frozen	6tbsps peas, fresh or frozen
6 × 15ml spoons corn kernels, fresh or frozen	6tbsps corn kernels, fresh or frozen
½ small cabbage, shredded	½ small cabbage, shredded
Approx. 175g cooked beetroot, diced, fresh or frozen	Approx. 6oz cooked beetroot, diced, fresh or frozen
125g sliced frankfurters or browned and sliced bratwurst	4oz sliced frankfurters or browned and sliced bratwurst

This is a thick, hearty, colourful vegetable soup which is almost a meal on its own, especially when served with rye bread.

Melt the butter, add prepared onion, carrots, turnip or swede, celery, potatoes and leek and toss until butter is absorbed. Add the stock and seasoning and simmer 20 minutes. Add peas, corn kernels and cabbage and simmer a further 15 minutes. Add beetroot and sausages, heat a further 5 minutes only and then serve.

To freeze See page 20. Add cabbage, beetroot and frankfurters on reheating.

Serves 6

Stuffed Globe Artichokes*

Metric	Imperial
4 large artichokes	4 large artichokes
225g cooked ham, finely minced	½lb cooked ham, finely minced
1 clove garlic, crushed, optional	1 clove garlic, crushed, optional
1 onion, chopped and lightly fried	1 onion, chopped and lightly fried
50g fresh breadcrumbs	2oz fresh breadcrumbs
1 × 1.25ml spoon dried herbs	¼tsp dried herbs
Salt and pepper	Salt and pepper
1 egg yolk	1 egg yolk
White wine or cider	White wine or cider
150ml tomato juice	¼ pint tomato juice

Use large artichokes for stuffing.

Trim off the rough, lower leaves and cut off the stalk as close as possible to the flower so the artichoke will stand upright. Trim off tops of other leaves with scissors. Put into a pan of boiling, salted water and simmer 10–15 minutes, according to size. Drain and plunge into cold water. When cool enough to handle cut into halves and remove the chokes (i.e. hairy centre reached by separating the central leaves of the artichokes). Make stuffing by mixing the ham, garlic, onion, breadcrumbs, herbs and seasoning, adding the egg yolk and enough wine or cider to moisten. Put in the place of the chokes. Tie each artichoke into shape with string and stand in a greased dish just large enough to hold them. Mix the tomato juice with an equal quantity of wine or cider and pour over. Cover with a lid or foil and bake at 180°C/350°F, Gas Mark 4 for about 45 minutes or until tender. Serve hot.

To freeze Reduce cooking time to 30 minutes, cool quickly and freeze in a rigid container.

To serve Thaw overnight in the refrigerator or transfer to original dish, put into a cold oven and reheat for about 30 minutes at temperature given above.

Serves 4

Grilled Grapefruit Medley

Metric	Imperial
2 grapefruit	2 grapefruit
50g brown sugar	2oz brown sugar
4 × 5ml spoons brandy	4tsps brandy
15g butter	½oz butter
50g sultanas	2oz sultanas
25g crystallized or glacé cherries, halved	1oz crystallized or glacé cherries, halved
1 × 1.25ml spoon ground cinnamon	¼tsp ground cinnamon

An excellent first course, serve this on a cold day.

Cut the grapefruit into halves, remove cores and loosen segments. Sprinkle with half the sugar and the brandy. Put under a hot grill until the brandy flares. At the same time heat the remaining ingredients together in a small pan. As the flames die down put each grapefruit half into a fruit dish and pile the dried fruit mixture on top. Serve at once.

Serves 4

Scotch Broth*

Metric	Imperial
1kg silverside	2lb silverside
1 litre cold water	2 pints cold water
Salt and pepper	Salt and pepper
25g barley, washed	1oz barley, washed
1 turnip, peeled and diced	1 turnip, peeled and diced
1 leek, diced	1 leek, diced
1 large onion, diced	1 large onion, diced
3 large carrots, peeled and quartered	3 large carrots, peeled and quartered
1 small swede or turnip, peeled and quartered	1 small swede or turnip, peeled and quartered
2–3 stalks celery, cut into 2cm lengths	2–3 stalks celery, cut into 1in lengths
Chopped parsley	Chopped parsley

Many countries have soups similar to this, in which meat for the main course is simmered in water with vegetables. In this version the vegetables to be served hot with the meat (except potatoes) are cooked in the liquid as well as the ones which are part of the broth.

Put the meat, water, seasoning and barley into a pan, bring to the boil and skim. Add the diced vegetables, cover and simmer for 2 hours. Add the remaining vegetables and simmer a further hour. Lift the meat and larger pieces of vegetable on to a heated dish and serve as the main course. Leave remaining vegetables in the liquid and serve as broth, sprinkling with chopped parsley. If liked, a small amount of shredded cabbage can be added for the last ½ hour. Neck of mutton can be used instead of silverside.

To freeze See general note on page 20.

Serves 4–5

Vegetarian Pâté

Metric	Imperial
3 small carrots, peeled and grated	3 small carrots, peeled and grated
1 very small onion, grated	1 very small onion, grated
1 small green pepper, seeded and chopped	1 small green pepper, seeded and chopped
50g small mushrooms, chopped	2oz small mushrooms, chopped
50g chopped nuts	2oz chopped nuts
1 inner stalk celery and its leaves, chopped	1 inner stalk celery and its leaves, chopped
Small piece firm turnip, peeled and grated	Small piece of firm turnip, peeled and grated
Grated rind of 1 small orange	Grated rind of 1 small orange
Salt and pepper	Salt and pepper
1 × 5ml spoon Worcestershire sauce	1tsp Worcestershire sauce
Good pinch cayenne pepper	Good pinch cayenne pepper
15g powdered unflavoured gelatine	½oz powdered unflavoured gelatine
3 × 15ml spoons orange juice	3tbsps orange juice

A colourful paté, this has an interesting orange flavour.

Mix together the carrots, onion, green pepper, mushrooms, nuts, celery, turnip and orange rind. Season with salt, pepper, sauce and cayenne pepper. Dissolve the gelatine in the orange juice and mix in. Divide between 4 small lightly oiled dishes. Turn out when set and serve with hot buttered toast.

Serves 4

Fruits Vinaigrette*

Metric	Imperial
Vinaigrette:	Vinaigrette:
1 × 5ml spoon castor sugar	1tsp castor sugar
Salt and freshly ground black pepper	Salt and freshly ground black pepper
Good pinch dry mustard or 1 × 1.25ml spoon prepared French mustard	Good pinch dry mustard or ¼tsp prepared French mustard
1 × 15ml spoon wine vinegar	1tbsp wine vinegar
3–4 × 15ml spoons olive oil	3–4tbsps olive oil
1 × 15ml spoon chopped fresh herbs, see method	1tbsp chopped fresh herbs, see method

Fruit: In summer and autumn choose from fresh pears, peaches, plums and melons. Oranges and grapefruit are available throughout the year and so are grapes, which are best mixed with other fruits. The fruits chosen should be as near ripe perfection as possible. Frozen fruit can be used and is best thawed in the refrigerator and dressed while still very cold. Drain if necessary.

Use either one type of fruit or a mixture for this very refreshing first course.

Put sugar, salt, pepper, mustard and vinegar into a basin and mix with a wooden spoon until sugar dissolves. Add the oil, a little at a time, until well blended. (Herb oils and/or vinegars can be used.) Stir in the herbs. These can be fresh or frozen. Use mint, parsley or chervil, chives, thyme, tarragon, marjoram and basil, using either just one herb or a mixture of two or three. Have the dressing ready before preparing the fruit. *Preparation* Pears and peaches should be peeled and the cores or stones discarded; cut melon into balls or cubes; cut oranges and grapefruit into sections or slices after peeling, and grapes peel and seed. For fruit salad cut fruit into smaller pieces. Add immediately to the dressing to prevent discoloration. Serve in small glasses or, as appropriate, orange or grapefruit shells with herb bread (see page 70).

To freeze Pack into rigid polythene containers. Cover, seal and freeze.

To serve Thaw overnight in a refrigerator or at room temperature for 3–4 hours. Stir carefully before serving.

Serves 4

Summer Vegetable Soup

Metric
600ml yogurt
½ large cucumber, coarsely grated
2 tomatoes, skinned, seeded and chopped
1 medium carrot, peeled and grated
50g peas, fresh or frozen, cooked
2–3 spring onions, chopped
2 × 15ml spoons finely chopped mint
5 × 15ml spoons single cream
Salt and freshly ground white pepper
Approx. 300ml strong, fat-free, chicken stock
Garnish:
Hard-boiled egg, finely chopped
Spring onion curls

Imperial
1 pint yogurt
½ large cucumber, coarsely grated
2 tomatoes, skinned, seeded and chopped
1 medium carrot, peeled and grated
2oz peas, fresh or frozen, cooked
2–3 spring onions, chopped
2tbsps finely chopped mint
5tbsps single cream
Salt and freshly ground white pepper
Approx. ½ pint strong, fat-free chicken stock
Garnish:
Hard-boiled egg, finely chopped
Spring onion curls

Yogurt gives a sharp flavour to this soup which is very refreshing in hot weather.

Mix all the ingredients in the order given, adding enough stock to give the consistency of thick cream. Chill well. Serve in individual dishes, garnishing each with a little chopped hard-boiled egg and one or two spring onion curls. This soup will not freeze.

Serves 4

Cauliflower Soup*

Metric
1 medium to large cauliflower
15g butter
600ml chicken or veal stock
Salt and white pepper
15g cornflour
150ml milk
1 egg yolk
3 × 15ml spoons single cream
Garnish:
Flaked browned almonds
Chopped chives

Imperial
1 medium to large cauliflower
½oz butter
1 pint chicken or veal stock
Salt and white pepper
½oz cornflour
¼ pint milk
1 egg yolk
3tbsps single cream
Garnish:
Flaked browned almonds
Chopped chives

This soup has a delicate flavour and so is an ideal start to a fairly elaborate meal.

Break the cauliflower into florets, wash and drain well. Melt the butter, add cauliflower and toss to absorb the butter without browning. Add stock and seasoning, cover and simmer for 20 minutes. Remove one floret and divide into very small sprigs. Put contents of pan into blender and liquidize until smooth. Return to the rinsed pan and heat. Mix the cornflour to a smooth paste with the milk and add to the soup. Bring to the boil and boil, stirring, for 3 minutes. Mix egg yolk and cream, add to the soup and heat, without boiling, to cook the egg. Adjust the seasoning and add the retained sprigs. Garnish each bowl of soup with a few flaked almonds and with chopped chives.

To freeze See general note on page 20.

Serves 4

Pears with Tarragon and Cream*

Metric
2 ripe pears
1 egg
2 × 15ml spoons tarragon vinegar
2 × 5ml spoons caster sugar
3 × 15ml spoons whipped cream
Lettuce leaves
Paprika

Imperial
2 ripe pears
1 egg
2tbsps tarragon vinegar
2tsps caster sugar
3tbsps whipped cream
Lettuce leaves
Paprika

Serve this first course when you have pears completely ripe but not over-ripe. The tarragon and cream dressing can be frozen ready to add to the pears.

Chill the pears in the refrigerator for 1 hour or longer. Put the egg, vinegar and sugar into a small pan and mix well. Put over a low heat and stir, without boiling, until the mixture thickens. Stand the pan in cold water to cool quickly and stir occasionally. When quite cold, fold in the cream. Just before serving, peel, halve and core the pears. Put each half, cut side down, on a crisp lettuce leaf. Coat at once with the dressing, sprinkle a little paprika on top and serve.

To freeze dressing As this is the smallest amount which can be made at one time some will be left over. Put into a very small container, seal and freeze.

To use Thaw at room temperature for 1–2 hours.

Serves 4

Jerusalem Artichoke Soup*

Metric
450g Jerusalem artichokes
25g butter
1 onion, chopped
600ml chicken or veal stock
Salt and white pepper
15g cornflour
150ml milk
150ml single cream
Garnish:
Fried croûtons of bread

Imperial
1lb Jerusalem artichokes
1oz butter
1 onion, chopped
1 pint chicken or veal stock
Salt and white pepper
½oz cornflour
¼ pint milk
¼ pint single cream
Garnish:
Fried croûtons of bread

This rather delicately flavoured soup is ideal as the first course of a dinner.

Prepare the artichokes by peeling as thinly as possible, cutting into pieces and putting each at once into cold water with a little lemon juice or vinegar added, to preserve the colour. Melt the butter and toss prepared artichokes and onion until the fat is absorbed, but do not allow the vegetables to colour. Add the stock and seasoning, bring to the boil and simmer for about 45 minutes until the vegetables are soft. Put into blender or rub through a non-metal sieve. Return to the rinsed pan with the cornflour mixed until dissolved with the milk. Bring to the boil, simmer and stir for 3 minutes. Remove from heat, cool a fraction and then stir in cream. Garnish each bowl with a few fried croûtons of bread or serve them separately.

To freeze See general note on page 20.
Serves 4–5

Mushrooms à la Grecque*

Metric
300ml water
1 small onion, chopped
2 × 15ml spoons olive oil
1 × 5ml spoon tomato purée
Salt and pepper
Bouquet garni
Juice of ½ lemon
350g small button mushrooms
Garnish:
Chopped parsley
Lemon wedges

Imperial
½ pint water
1 small onion, chopped
2tbsps olive oil
1tsp tomato purée
Salt and pepper
Bouquet garni
Juice of ½ lemon
¾lb small button mushrooms
Garnish:
Chopped parsley
Lemon wedges

A savoury way of serving mushrooms or other vegetables as a first course, this can be prepared well in advance.

Put the water, onion, oil, purée, seasoning, herbs and lemon juice into a pan and simmer 5 minutes. Trim off ends of mushroom stalks and wipe mushrooms with a damp cloth. Add to liquid and simmer 10 minutes. Remove with a slotted spoon. Boil liquid rapidly until it is reduced to 3–4 × 15ml spoons (3–4tbsps), removing herbs when about half the liquid remains. Pour over mushrooms and chill. Just before serving, sprinkle lavishly with chopped parsley and add a lemon wedge to each serving.

To freeze Put into a rigid container, ungarnished, seal and freeze.
To serve Thaw 6 hours, or longer, in the refrigerator and garnish before serving.

Alternative vegetables: artichoke hearts, aubergine, celery, chicory, cucumber, fennel, leeks, small onions, pepper quarters. Prepare in the same way, simmering, if necessary for a longer time, until the vegetables are cooked.

Serves 4–5

Tomato and Mint Soup*

Metric
25g butter
1 carrot, peeled and cubed
1 onion, chopped
3 stalks celery, chopped
50g bacon pieces, chopped
Few bacon rinds
¾kg tomatoes, chopped
750ml stock
Salt and pepper
1–2 × 5ml spoons sugar, or to taste
2 × 15ml spoons chopped fresh mint
15g cornflour
150ml milk
Garnish:
A few mint leaves

Imperial
1oz butter
1 carrot, peeled and cubed
1 onion, chopped
3 stalks of celery, chopped
2oz bacon pieces, chopped
Few bacon rinds
1½lb tomatoes, chopped
1¼ pints stock
Salt and pepper
1–2tsps sugar, or to taste
2tbsps chopped fresh mint
½oz cornflour
¼ pint milk
Garnish:
A few mint leaves

A very good soup for the vegetable gardener, this can be made when tomatoes and mint are at their best together.

Melt the butter and toss in the prepared carrot, onion, celery and bacon until butter is absorbed. Add bacon rinds and tomatoes. Cook 2 minutes, then add stock, seasoning, sugar and mint. (The amount of sugar will depend upon the tomatoes so add some at this stage and taste for sweetness later.) Cover and simmer for 45 minutes. Rub through a sieve (more flavour is obtained if the soup is put into the blender first). Return to rinsed pan, add cornflour mixed to a smooth paste with milk and boil, stirring, for 3 minutes. Test for seasoning. Garnish each bowl of soup with 2 or 3 mint leaves. It can also be served cold adding also a little soured cream.

To freeze See general note on page 20.
Serves 4–5

Nineteenth-century Poacher's Broth*

Metric
1 large rabbit
Small piece salt pork
1.8 litres cold water
2 onions, roughly chopped
Pepper
225g potatoes, peeled and diced
225g kale, finely shredded
Garnish:
1 medium onion, sliced and pushed out into rings

Imperial
1 large rabbit
Small piece salt pork
3 pints cold water
2 onions, roughly chopped
Pepper
½lb potatoes, peeled and diced
½lb kale, finely shredded
Garnish:
1 medium onion, sliced and pushed out into rings

The ingredients for this broth are readily available to the vegetable gardener, except, of course, the rabbit. If this proves difficult, substitute boiling fowl.

Cut the rabbit into serving portions, put into a pan with the salt pork, cover with cold water and bring to the boil. Discard this water, add the measured cold water, onions and pepper. Bring to the boil and simmer 1½ hours. Remove rabbit and salt pork. Add the potatoes and kale. Cook a further 20–30 minutes. Meanwhile, reserve the meaty joints of hind legs and back of rabbit for a later meal, remove meat from the other joints, cut into dice and add to the broth with the lean meat from the pork, also diced. Serve hot with 2 or 3 raw onion rings in each dish.
To freeze See general note below.
Serves 8

Individual Spinach Soufflés

Metric
15g butter
15g flour
125g spinach purée
3 × 15ml spoons single cream
Salt, pepper and grated nutmeg
50g grated cheese
2 eggs, separated

Imperial
½oz butter
½oz flour
4oz spinach purée
3tbsps single cream
Salt, pepper and grated nutmeg
2oz grated cheese
2 eggs, separated

This is an elegant starter for an evening meal.

Melt the butter, stir in the flour and cook for a few minutes. Add the spinach purée (which must be well drained and quite dry) and, when blended, the cream and seasonings. Cook and stir carefully for a few minutes until very thick, then remove from heat. Stir in the cheese and then the yolks, one at a time. Whisk egg whites until very stiff and fold in with a metal spoon. Divide between 4 individual, greased soufflé dishes and bake at 200°C/400°F, Gas Mark 6 for 15–20 minutes until well-risen and set. Serve at once.
Serves 4

Sweetcorn Chowder*

Metric
50g streaky bacon, diced
½ small onion, diced
3 potatoes, peeled and cubed
300ml boiling water
Salt and pepper
450g corn kernels, fresh or frozen
15g cornflour
900ml milk
Garnish:
Cooked peas

Imperial
2oz streaky bacon, diced
½ small onion, diced
3 potatoes, peeled and cubed
½ pint boiling water
Salt and pepper
1lb corn kernels, fresh or frozen
½oz cornflour
1½ pints milk
Garnish:
Cooked peas

Chowder is a thick soup usually containing either salt pork or bacon and potatoes. It can be described as a 'meal soup' if small pieces of meat or fish are added.

Fry the bacon in a strong pan and, as the fat runs, add onion and fry about 5 minutes without browning. Add prepared potatoes, water and seasoning, cover and cook for 15 minutes. Add corn and cook a further 5 minutes. Mix the cornflour to a smooth paste with some of the milk and add to chowder with remaining milk. Bring to the boil and cook and stir for 5 minutes. Serve hot garnished with peas.
To freeze See general note below.
Serves 4–5

General Notes on Freezing Soups

With freezer space usually at a premium it is an advantage to freeze soups in a condensed form whenever possible. This is done by following the recipe but adding only enough measured stock or water barely to cover the vegetables and any other ingredients such as meat. If given in the recipe, put through the blender or rub through a sieve. *Do not add cornflour or egg yolk for thickening.* Freeze in smallest possible container, marking plainly the amount of liquid still to be added and the thickening needed.
To reheat Put frozen soup into a pan with the extra liquid and heat. When all is melted, finish as given in the recipe.

Main Course Dishes

Turnips and Gammon

Metric
¾kg new turnips, peeled and
   cut into 1cm cubes
15g butter
350–450g thick slice of
   gammon cut into 1cm cubes
Freshly ground black pepper
2 × 15ml spoons chopped
   parsley
2–3 × 15ml spoons single
   cream or top-of-the-milk
Garnish:
Mushrooms and small
   tomatoes, grilled or baked

Imperial
1½lb new turnips, peeled and
   cut into ½in cubes
½oz butter
¾–1lb thick slice of gammon,
   cut into 1in cubes
Freshly ground black pepper
2 tbsps chopped parsley
2–3tbsps single cream or
   top-of-the-milk
Garnish:
Mushrooms and small
   tomatoes, grilled or baked

A deceptively simple dish, this is absolutely delicious to eat, especially when you can dig up the turnips just before you want them.
Boil the prepared turnips in salted water for 10–15 minutes or until just cooked, then drain. Meanwhile, melt the butter and fry the gammon dice slowly until cooked, then add the turnip and pepper and toss carefully together for 5 minutes. Stir in the parsley and cream, reheat and pile into the centre of a heated serving dish. Surround with the mushrooms and tomatoes.
Serves 4

Cabbage and Sausage Casserole

Metric
3 rashers streaky bacon,
   rinded and chopped
1 medium onion, chopped
½ large cooking apple, peeled,
   cored and chopped
450–575g savoy cabbage,
   shredded
450g pork sausages (8)
Garnish:
Small potatoes
Parsley or other herb butter

Imperial
3 rashers streaky bacon
   rinded and chopped
1 medium onion, chopped
½ large cooking apple, peeled,
   cored and chopped
1–1¼lb savoy cabbage,
   shredded
1lb pork sausages (8)
Garnish:
Small potatoes
Parsley or other herb butter

Try this very good way of making an inexpensive but tasty dish from cabbage during the winter months.
Fry the bacon until the fat begins to flow and then add and fry the onion and the apple. Wash and drain prepared cabbage, add to pan and cook about 5 minutes. Transfer to an oblong baking dish. Fry the sausages for about 3 minutes to start them cooking, then put on the cabbage, and cook at 200°C/400°F, Gas Mark 6 for 30 minutes.
   Cook the potatoes in the usual way, drain, toss in parsley or other herb butter and arrange round the sausages.
Serves 4–6

Mediterranean-style Veal Chops*

Metric
25g butter
1 × 15ml spoon oil
4 veal chops
Salt and freshly ground black
   pepper
350g mushrooms, sliced
2 large green or red peppers,
   seeded and sliced
350g tomatoes, skinned and
   sliced
1 × 15ml spoon chopped fresh
   basil
1 × 5ml spoon sugar
300ml chicken stock or water

Imperial
1oz butter
1tbsp oil
4 veal chops
Salt and freshly ground black
   pepper
¾lb mushrooms, sliced
2 large green or red peppers,
   seeded and sliced
¾lb tomatoes, skinned and
   sliced
1tbsp chopped fresh basil
1tsp sugar
½ pint chicken stock or water

Melt the butter and oil together and fry the chops, quickly, until browned on both sides; season and remove from pan. Fry the prepared mushrooms and peppers until soft, add the tomatoes, seasoning, basil, sugar and stock or water. Boil for 3 minutes. Return chops to the pan and simmer, uncovered, for about 30 minutes. The sauce should be very thick. Arrange the chops on a heated dish with the sauce and garnish with lemon wedges.
To freeze Cool quickly after 20 minutes simmering, pack into rigid containers, seal, label and freeze.
To serve Thaw overnight in a refrigerator or put, unthawed, into a strong pan and heat slowly until thawed. Simmer for 10 minutes and serve as above.
Serves 4

Mediterranean-style veal chops with a potato border

Chakchouka

Metric	Imperial
2 × 15ml spoons olive oil	2tbsps olive oil
2 medium onions, sliced	2 medium onions, sliced
4 medium green peppers, seeded and sliced	4 medium green peppers, seeded and sliced
Salt and pepper	Salt and pepper
Good pinch cayenne pepper	Good pinch cayenne pepper
1 × 1.25ml spoon chilli powder	¼tsp chilli powder
2 or 4 small to medium tomatoes, halved	2 or 4 small to medium tomatoes, halved
4–8 eggs	4–8 eggs

Chakchouka is the North African name for a vegetable dish which, in one form or another, is popular in all the Arab countries surrounding the Mediterranean.

Heat the oil, stir in the prepared onions and peppers and cook slowly in a covered pan until cooked. Season with salt, pepper, cayenne and chilli powder. Put the tomato halves on to the vegetables, put on the lid and cook for a further 3 minutes. The tomato halves should remain unbroken.

Divide the onions and peppers between 4 individual dishes and make a hollow in each. Put the tomato halves on the edges. Break one or two eggs per person into the hollows, season the eggs and bake at 200°C/400°F, Gas Mark 6 for 7–10 minutes to set the eggs.

Variations The amount of cayenne and chilli powder can be adjusted to taste. Also, the eggs can be dropped whole into the pan and cooked there or, when partly cooked, the yolks can be broken with a wooden spoon and stirred into the vegetables.

Serves 4

Chicken Divan

Metric	Imperial
50g butter	2oz butter
25g flour	1oz flour
Salt and pepper	Salt and pepper
400ml mixed stock and milk	Scant ¾ pint mixed stock and milk
125g grated cheese	4oz grated cheese
1 × 5ml spoon minced or grated onion	1tsp minced or grated onion
3 × 15ml spoons dry sherry	3tbsps dry sherry
125ml whipped double cream, optional	4floz whipped double cream, optional
450g broccoli, fresh or frozen, cooked and drained, or calabrese	1lb broccoli, fresh or frozen, cooked and drained, or calabrese
350–450g cooked chicken (or turkey), sliced	¾–1lb cooked chicken (or turkey), sliced
Extra 50g grated cheese	Extra 2oz grated cheese

This American dish shows a very tasty way of serving left-over cooked chicken (or turkey), again as a hot dish.

Melt the butter in a saucepan. Stir in the flour and cook for 1 minute, then stir in the seasoning and stock and milk. Bring to the boil and simmer, stirring, until thick and smooth. Add the cheese, onion and sherry. Stir in the whipped cream, if used. Put the cooked broccoli into a flameproof dish and coat with half of the sauce. Cover with the chicken slices, the remaining sauce and the extra cheese, in that order. Put under a grill on low heat until the chicken is hot, then turn up heat to brown.

Serves 4

Vegetable and Frankfurter Pie

Metric	Imperial
225g cooked mixed vegetables	½lb cooked mixed vegetables
Salt and freshly ground black pepper	Salt and freshly ground black pepper
25g butter or herb butter	1oz butter or herb butter
225g frankfurters	½lb frankfurters
225g cooked potatoes, sliced	½lb cooked potatoes, sliced
225g tomatoes, skinned and sliced	½lb tomatoes, skinned and sliced
1 × 2.5ml spoon sugar	½tsp sugar
Puff pastry made from 250g flour and 65g fat	Puff pastry made from 5oz flour and 2½oz fat
Beaten egg	Beaten egg

This is an excellent way of using up left-over cooked vegetables or the remainder of several different frozen vegetable packs.

Put the cooked vegetables into a 700–900ml (1¼–1½ pint) pie dish. Season and add half the butter in small flakes. Cut the frankfurters into halves lengthways and then across (into quarters). Arrange over the vegetables, cover with the potatoes and then the tomatoes. Season, sprinkle with the sugar and the remaining butter in flakes. Roll out the pastry until little larger than the pie dish and cut out a circle following the outside rim of the dish. Moisten pastry or brush with egg and fit on top. Seal, trim and 'knock up' the edges. Make a hole in the centre for steam to escape and decorate with leaves cut from the pastry trimmings. Glaze with the beaten egg and bake for 40 minutes at 200°C/400°F, Gas Mark 6. Serve hot.

Serves 4

Beans and Eggs au Gratin

Metric
450g shelled broad beans,
  fresh or frozen
2–3 hard-boiled eggs, sliced
40g butter
40g flour
400ml creamy milk
Salt and cayenne pepper
Topping:
15g butter
25g fresh breadcrumbs
50g grated cheese

Imperial
1lb shelled broad beans,
  fresh or frozen
2–3 hard-boiled eggs, sliced
1½oz butter
1½oz flour
¾ pint creamy milk
Salt and cayenne pepper
Topping:
½oz butter
1oz fresh breadcrumbs
2oz grated cheese

A delicious supper or high tea dish, serve this in winter when your frozen broad beans will be doubly welcome.
Cook the beans in salted water until just soft. Drain. Layer the beans and eggs in a baking dish, having beans as top and bottom layers. Make a sauce from the butter, flour and milk, and season with salt and cayenne pepper. Pour over the beans. For the topping, melt the butter and add the breadcrumbs and cheese. When mixed, sprinkle over the sauce. Bake at 220°C/425°F, Gas Mark 7 for 15 minutes or until the topping is browned and crisped.
Variations 1. Use small, whole French beans.
2. Drain 198g (7oz) can tuna, flake and layer with the sliced eggs.
3. Use minced cooked meats or poultry and layer with the eggs.
4. Reserve some egg slices for garnish.
Serves 4–6

Pipérade*

Metric
50g butter
1 × 15ml spoon oil
125g onions, sliced
125g red or green peppers,
  seeded and sliced
2 cloves garlic, crushed
3 large tomatoes, skinned,
  seeded and chopped
Salt and pepper
4 eggs
2 × 15ml spoons milk
Garnish:
Parsley, chopped
Toast
Garlic butter

Imperial
2oz butter
1tbsp oil
4oz onions, sliced
4oz red or green peppers,
  seeded and sliced
2 cloves garlic, crushed
3 large tomatoes, skinned,
  seeded and chopped
Salt and pepper
4 eggs
2tbsps milk
Garnish:
Parsley, chopped
Toast
Garlic butter

A savoury and colourful vegetable and egg dish from the Basque countryside, serve it at luncheon or supper or take it cold on a picnic.
Melt the fats and fry the onions, without colouring, until almost soft. Add peppers and, after 5 minutes, the garlic and tomatoes. Season, and simmer until all ingredients are soft and most of the liquid from the tomatoes has evaporated. Beat eggs, milk and seasoning and scramble lightly, separately. Turn the vegetables on to a heated dish, spread the eggs on top and fork a little of the vegetables into the edges of the egg. Sprinkle with chopped parsley and surround with small triangles of toast spread with garlic butter.
Variations
1. Add grilled rashers of back bacon or gammon for a more substantial dish.
2. Cut the end off a French loaf, remove crumbs and replace with cold piperade, for a picnic dish.
3. Use to stuff tomatoes and serve hot or cold.
To freeze When vegetable ingredients are soft, cool quickly, pack, label and seal.
To serve Thaw overnight in the refrigerator or put, still frozen, into a strong pan over a low heat until thawed. Scramble eggs, etc. as above.
Serves 4

Spinach Luncheon Casserole

Metric
1kg spinach, cooked and
  drained
Salt and pepper
Juice of ½ lemon
125g cooked ham or gammon,
  chopped
25g butter
175g mushrooms
2 eggs
125g grated cheese
2 × 15ml spoons single cream
  or top-of-the-milk

Imperial
2lb spinach, cooked and
  drained
Salt and pepper
Juice of ½ lemon
4oz cooked ham or gammon,
  chopped
1oz butter
6oz mushrooms
2 eggs
4oz grated cheese
2tbsps single cream or
  top-of-the-milk

Like Eggs Florentine, make this dish with fresh spinach as given in the recipe, or with frozen spinach, already chopped.
Season the drained spinach with salt, pepper and lemon juice. Mix in the cooked ham or gammon and put into a greased ovenproof dish. Melt the butter, cook the mushrooms in it and then arrange them on top of the spinach. Beat the eggs with salt and pepper, add the cheese and cream or top-of-the-milk, and pour over the mushrooms. Bake for 25 minutes at 200°C/400°F, Gas Mark 6.
Serves 4

Onions with Sausagemeat*

Metric	Imperial
4 large Spanish-type onions	4 large Spanish-type onions
25g butter	1oz butter
1 × 1.25ml spoon dried mixed herbs or marjoram	¼tsp dried mixed herbs or marjoram
Salt and freshly ground black pepper	Salt and freshly ground black pepper
225g pork sausagemeat	½lb pork sausagemeat
2 × 15ml spoons fresh breadcrumbs	2tbsps fresh breadcrumbs
1 × 15ml spoon Worcestershire sauce	1tbsp Worcestershire sauce
Small whole tomatoes	Small whole tomatoes

Often, when onions are stuffed and baked, the outside layer of onion is overcooked, or the whole onion comes apart. This method prevents such results.

Wash the unskinned onions and, very carefully, trim the root ends so the onions will stand upright but be careful not to remove more than is necessary. Put into a pan of cold water, bring to the boil, reduce the heat and simmer 15 minutes. Drain and rinse in cold water until cool enough to handle. Cut a slice from the top of each onion and discard its brown skin. Remove most of the insides from the onions, leaving a two-layer thickness all round. Chop the removed onion and cook in the butter for a few minutes. Add the herbs, seasoning and sausagemeat. Break up with a fork and fry until the sausagemeat is lightly browned. Add the breadcrumbs and Worcestershire sauce. Use to stuff the onions and pile on top. Any extra should be placed in a greased baking dish. Stand the onions in the dish and bake at 200°C/400°F, Gas Mark 6 for 20 minutes. Garnish with whole small tomatoes baked in the oven at the same time as the onions. The brown skins are easily removed at table.

To freeze Freeze immediately after stuffing.

To serve Thaw in the refrigerator overnight or in the kitchen for 3 hours, then bake as above.

Serves 4

Chicory au Gratin

Metric	Imperial
8 heads of chicory	8 heads of chicory
Lemon juice	Lemon juice
50–125g grated cheese	2–4oz grated cheese
25g butter	1oz butter
25g fresh white breadcrumbs	1oz fresh white breadcrumbs

This can be served when only a light course is required or, with the addition of bacon or gammon, can be made into a more substantial lunch or supper dish.

Trim the chicory and, with a pointed knife, hollow out the hard core at the bottom. Cook in boiling salted water, adding a few drops of lemon juice to keep the chicory white, for 20 minutes. Drain well. Put into a greased flameproof dish and sprinkle with the cheese. Melt the butter, mix in the breadcrumbs and sprinkle on top. Brown under a hot grill or in a hot oven.

To make a more substantial dish put slices of freshly cooked bacon or gammon underneath the chicory or wrap each piece of chicory in a slice of cooked ham before sprinkling with cheese, etc.

Serves 4

Nut and Vegetable Loaf

Metric	Imperial
15g butter or fat	½oz butter or fat
1 small onion, chopped	1 small onion, chopped
1 small carrot, peeled and chopped	1 small carrot, peeled and chopped
1 stalk celery, chopped	1 stalk celery, chopped
2 × 5ml spoons tomato purée	2tsps tomato purée
225g tomatoes, skinned and chopped	½lb tomatoes, skinned and chopped
2 eggs	2 eggs
1 × 5ml spoon dried thyme	1tsp dried thyme
Salt and pepper	Salt and pepper
225g chopped or minced nuts	½lb chopped or minced nuts

Melt the fat and cook prepared onion, carrot and celery until soft, then add the tomato purée and tomatoes and cook for 5 minutes. Put the eggs into a basin with herbs and seasoning; beat well. Stir in the nuts and then the vegetables. Transfer to a greased loaf tin approx. 20 × 11.5cm (8 × 4½in) or ovenproof dish, and bake for 25–30 minutes at 220°C/425°F, Gas Mark 7. Turn out and, if liked, decorate with onion rings and parsley. Serve hot with vegetables and a sauce or gravy, or cold with salad.

Serves 4–6

Stuffed Cauliflower

Metric	Imperial
1 large cauliflower	1 large cauliflower
Filling:	*Filling:*
50g rice	2oz rice
25g butter	1oz butter
1 medium onion, chopped	1 medium onion, chopped
225g minced steak	½lb minced steak
225g tomatoes, skinned and chopped	½lb tomatoes, skinned and chopped
63g tin tomato purée	2¼oz tin tomato purée
Salt, pepper and sugar	Salt, pepper and sugar
1 × 15ml spoon chopped fresh basil	1tbsp chopped fresh basil
Sauce:	*Sauce:*
400ml milk	¾ pint milk
50g mushrooms, sliced	2oz mushrooms, sliced
25g butter	1oz butter
25g flour	1oz flour
Dry mustard	Dry mustard
125g grated cheese	4oz grated cheese

Boil the cauliflower in salted water until *almost* cooked. Boil the rice and drain. Melt the butter, fry the onion and then the meat, breaking it up with a fork. When evenly browned, add tomatoes, tomato purée, salt, pepper, a pinch of sugar and the basil. Simmer 10 minutes, then stir in the rice. Heat the milk and mushrooms together and simmer until the mushrooms are tender. Melt the fat and stir in the flour. Cook, stirring, for 1 minute, then stir in the mustard, seasoning and milk and mushrooms. Bring to the boil and simmer, stirring, until thick. Stir in three-quarters of the cheese.

Put the whole cauliflower into a baking dish and cut downwards, *almost* into four quarters. Put the filling into the cuts, opening them out a little to take it all. Coat each quarter with its share of the sauce, sprinkle with remaining cheese and bake for 20 minutes at 200°C/400°F, Gas Mark 6 to brown lightly.

Serves 4

Eggs Florentine

Metric	Imperial
1kg prepared spinach, cooked and drained	2lb prepared spinach, cooked and drained
25g butter	1oz butter
Salt and pepper	Salt and pepper
A little freshly grated nutmeg	A little freshly grated nutmeg
4–8 eggs, poached	4–8 eggs, poached
Sauce:	*Sauce:*
25g butter	1oz butter
25g flour	1oz flour
300ml milk	½ pint milk
Pinch dry mustard	Pinch dry mustard
75g grated cheese	3oz grated cheese
Little extra cheese	Little extra cheese

This combination of spinach, egg and cheese works very well indeed and is one of the classic spinach dishes.

Chop the spinach finely and drain again. Set aside. To make the cheese sauce: melt butter in pan over low heat, stir in flour and make smooth paste. Cook together for one minute before slowly adding milk, stirring all the time until sauce thickens. Add seasoning, stir in grated cheese until completely melted. Reheat spinach in the butter and add salt, pepper and nutmeg to taste. Divide between four individual dishes, or use one large flameproof dish, and put on 1 or 2 poached eggs for each person. Coat with the cheese sauce, sprinkle a little cheese on top, and brown quickly under a hot grill.

For variety use baked, flaked fish fillets or slices of hot, cooked chicken instead of eggs.

Serves 4

Vegetable and Noodle Casserole

Metric	Imperial
1 × 400g can tomatoes, drained	1 × 14oz can tomatoes, drained
2 stalks celery, chopped	2 stalks celery, chopped
1 medium parsnip, peeled and chopped	1 medium parsnip, peeled and chopped
2 carrots, peeled and sliced	2 carrots, peeled and sliced
1 small swede, peeled and chopped	1 small swede, peeled and chopped
225g courgettes, sliced	½lb courgettes, sliced
1 pepper, seeded and sliced	1 pepper, seeded and sliced
1 bulb fennel, chopped	1 bulb fennel, chopped
1 large onion, sliced	1 large onion, sliced
Bouquet garni of rosemary, lemon thyme, parsley	Bouquet garni of rosemary, lemon thyme, parsley
Salt and pepper	Salt and pepper
2 × 15ml spoons tomato purée	2tbsps tomato purée
150ml dry white wine	¼ pint dry white wine
125g mushrooms	4oz mushrooms
50g noodles	2oz noodles

Put all the vegetables except the mushrooms in a large casserole dish. Add bouquet garni, salt and pepper and tomato purée. Pour in the wine and mix well. Cover with a tight-fitting lid and cook at 180°C/350°F, Gas Mark 4 for 2½ hours. Add the mushrooms after 2 hours. Cook the noodles in boiling salted water as directed on the packet, drain and add to the casserole 5 minutes before serving. Serve hot.

Serves 4

Pissaladière Niçoise

Metric	Imperial
Lightly cooked 20cm flan case of shortcrust pastry made from 200g flour and 90g fat	Lightly cooked 8in flan case of shortcrust pastry made from 7oz flour and 3½oz fat
¾kg onions, chopped	1½lb onions, chopped
4 × 15ml spoons oil	4tbsps oil
1 bouquet garni	1 bouquet garni
Salt and freshly ground black pepper	Salt and freshly ground black pepper
2 cloves garlic, crushed	2 cloves garlic, crushed
Anchovy fillets	Anchovy fillets
Black olives	Black olives

Sometimes a Pissaladière is made in a pastry flan case, as here, and sometimes, like a pizza, on a large round of bread dough.
Put the flan case on to a baking tray. Cook the onions slowly in 3 × 15ml spoons (3tbsps) oil with the herbs, salt and pepper for about 45 minutes. The onions should almost melt and acquire a rich golden colour. Stir in the garlic after about 20 minutes. Transfer to the pastry case and make a lattice pattern on top with the anchovies and olives. Sprinkle the remaining oil on top and bake at 200°C/400°F, Gas Mark 6 for 15 minutes or until really hot.
Serves 4

Potato Rings or Borders

Use these to make a main course look more attractive as well as providing at least part of the vegetables to be served with the meal. Potatoes alone can be used or they can be mixed with a variety of other vegetables—Jerusalem artichokes, cauliflower, carrot, celeriac, kohlrabi, parsnip, swede, turnip—in any proportion from equal quantities to 4 parts potato to 1 part of the other vegetable. The vegetables can be cooked together or separately, and should then be drained well and mashed until smooth. Reheat with a little fat such as butter or bacon fat, and adjust seasoning.
1. Form a border on a heated serving dish and fill with any type of stew, casserole, etc. of fish, meat, poultry or vegetables.
2. Form a shape on part of a large dish and surround with the stew etc. as above.
3. Form a straight strip against which chops can be placed.
4. Form rings as in 1. but on individual plates.

If only potatoes are used then beaten egg (about 1 egg to 1kg (2lb) potatoes) can be mixed in and the mixture used to line the sides and bottom of a 20.5cm (8in) loose-bottomed cake tin which has been greased and sprinkled with browned breadcrumbs. Bake at 220°C/425°F, Gas Mark 7 for about 30 minutes. Then carefully push up the base and slide the shape on to a heated plate. Fill and serve.

The potato mixture can also be made a little softer with the addition of a little more egg and piped into attractive shapes as duchesse potatoes.

Curried Stuffed Marrow

Metric	Imperial
1 × 15ml spoon oil	1tbsp oil
3 medium onions, diced	3 medium onions, diced
1 × 15ml spoon curry powder	1tbsp curry powder
2 × 15ml spoons flour	2tbsps flour
2 eating apples, peeled, cored and diced	2 eating apples, peeled, cored and diced
600ml homemade stock	1 pint homemade stock
2 × 15ml spoons chutney	2tbsps chutney
Salt and pepper	Salt and pepper
450g lamb, cooked and minced	1lb lamb, cooked and minced
1 medium marrow, halved and seeded	1 medium marrow, halved and seeded

Heat the oil in a pan and fry the onions until golden brown. Stir in the curry powder and cook for 2 minutes. Add the flour and cook for a further 2 minutes. Add the apples and gradually stir in the stock, mixing well. Bring to the boil and simmer for a few minutes. Add the chutney, season with salt and pepper, cover and simmer for 30 minutes.

Stir in the minced lamb. Put the mixture into the marrow halves and carefully place the marrow together again. Wrap in foil and place in a baking tin. Cook at 180°C/350°F, Gas Mark 4 for 45 minutes–1 hour until the marrow is tender but not overcooked. Serve sliced.
Serves 4–6

Supper Potato Cakes

Metric	Imperial
900g potatoes, cooked and mashed with 50g butter	2lb potatoes, cooked and mashed with 2oz butter
100g smoked sausage, sliced	4oz smoked sausage, sliced
1 small onion, chopped and fried	1 small onion, chopped and fried
Made mustard	Made mustard
50g cheese, sliced thinly	2oz cheese, sliced thinly
2 eggs, beaten	2 eggs, beaten
Fresh white breadcrumbs	Fresh white breadcrumbs
Deep fat to fry	Deep fat to fry

Form the potatoes into 16 ovals, each about 2.5 × 5cm (1 × 2in) in size. Top 4 with the smoked sausage slices, cover each with another oval and seal the edges. Top another 4 with the onion, spread with a little mustard and cover with the cheese. Cover with remaining ovals and seal edges. Coat all the potato cakes with beaten egg and breadcrumbs. Fry in deep fat until golden brown. Serve hot with Fresh Vegetable Sauce.
Serves 4

Savoury Stuffed Pancakes

Metric	Imperial
Batter:	*Batter:*
125g flour	4oz flour
Pinch of salt	Pinch of salt
1 egg	1 egg
300ml mixed milk and water	½ pint mixed milk and water
Oil for frying	Oil for frying
To finish:	*To finish:*
25g Parmesan cheese, grated	1oz Parmesan cheese, grated

Mix the flour and salt together in a bowl, make a well in the centre, drop in the egg, gradually add the liquid and beat well until smooth. Heat the oil in a frying pan, pour off any excess fat, spoon just enough batter into the pan to cover the base thinly, and cook quickly until golden brown underneath. Turn with a palette knife or toss, and cook the other side until golden. Keep the pancakes hot and fill with one of the fillings given below. Fold the pancakes into three, arrange in an ovenproof dish, sprinkle with the Parmesan cheese and cover with foil. Cook for 25–30 minutes at 180°C/350°F, Gas Mark 4, or until the pancakes are hot through. Serve at once. *Serves 4*

Chicken, Ham and Mushroom Filling:	
50g butter	2oz butter
125g mushrooms, sliced	4oz mushrooms, sliced
175g chicken, cooked and chopped	6oz chicken, cooked and chopped
175g cooked ham, minced	6oz cooked ham, minced
300ml double cream, whipped	½ pint double cream, whipped
1 × 5ml spoon chopped fresh savory	1tsp chopped fresh savory
1 clove garlic, crushed	1 clove garlic, crushed
Salt and pepper	Salt and pepper

Melt the butter in a pan, add the mushrooms and cook for 2 minutes. Remove from heat, stir in the chicken, ham, cream, savory and garlic, and season with salt and pepper. Warm gently, but do not boil.

Spinach Filling:	
450g spinach, cooked, drained and finely chopped	1lb spinach, cooked, drained and finely chopped
Salt and pepper	Salt and pepper
150ml double cream	¼ pint double cream

Mix all the ingredients together in a pan and warm gently but do not boil.

Seafood Filling:	
125g shelled prawns	4oz shelled prawns
2 scallops, diced	2 scallops, diced
125g shelled mussels	4oz shelled mussels
150ml dry white wine	¼ pint dry white wine
Bouquet garni	Bouquet garni
25g butter	1oz butter
25g flour	1oz flour
150ml milk	¼ pint milk
Salt and pepper	Salt and pepper
Fennel tops, chopped	Fennel tops, chopped

Poach shellfish in the wine with bouquet garni for 5 minutes. Drain, but reserve fish liquor. Remove the bouquet garni. Melt the butter in a pan, stir in the flour and cook for 2 minutes. Gradually add the fish liquor and milk and season with salt and pepper. Add the fennel tops and fish, bring to the boil and cook, stirring, for 2 minutes.

Stuffed Vine or Cabbage Leaves

Metric	Imperial
25g butter	1oz butter
450g lean minced lamb	1lb lean minced lamb
2 × 15ml spoons chopped parsley	2tbsps chopped parsley
2 × 15ml spoons chopped mint	2tbsps chopped mint
4 × 15ml spoons cooked rice	4tbsps cooked rice
1 onion, grated	1 onion, grated
1 × 5ml spoon mixed spice	1tsp mixed spice
150ml homemade stock	¼ pint homemade stock
12 vine or cabbage leaves	12 vine or cabbage leaves
Sauce:	*Sauce:*
1 small onion, finely chopped	1 small onion, finely chopped
1 clove garlic, crushed	1 clove garlic, crushed
1 × 15ml spoon oil	1tbsp oil
450g tomatoes, skinned and chopped	1lb tomatoes, skinned and chopped
2 × 15ml spoons tomato purée	2tbsps tomato purée
1 bayleaf	1 bayleaf
A bouquet garni	A bouquet garni
Dash of Worcestershire sauce	Dash of Worcestershire sauce
Salt and pepper	Salt and pepper
1 glass dry white wine	1 glass dry white wine

To make the tomato sauce: lightly fry the onion and garlic in the oil until transparent. Stir in the remaining ingredients, slowly bring to the boil, cover and simmer for 1–1½ hours. Remove the bouquet garni before serving.

Melt the butter in a pan, add the meat and cook until lightly browned. Add the parsley, mint, rice, onion, seasoning and mixed spice. Stir in the stock, and cook for 5–10 minutes until the stock is absorbed. Blanch the vine or cabbage leaves by cooking them in boiling water for 2 minutes; drain well. Place each leaf on the working surface, spoon filling in the centre of each leaf and roll up, tucking in the ends to form a neat parcel. Place the rolls close together in an ovenproof dish, and spoon over the tomato sauce to come halfway up the cabbage rolls. Cover with a lid or foil and cook in the centre of the oven at 180°C/350°F, Gas Mark 4, for 45 minutes. Serve the remaining sauce separately. *Serves 4*

Spanish Omelette

Metric
25g butter
1 clove garlic, crushed
1 small onion, chopped
1 tomato, skinned and chopped
2 potatoes, cooked and diced
1 small red pepper, seeded
  and chopped
2 × 15ml spoons peas, cooked
1 × 15ml spoon chopped
  parsley
4 eggs
Salt and pepper
Fresh herbs to serve

Imperial
1oz butter
1 clove garlic, erushed
1 small onion, chopped
1 tomato, skinned and chopped
2 potatoes, cooked and diced
1 small red pepper, seeded
  and chopped
2tbsps peas, cooked
1tbsp chopped parsley
4 eggs
Salt and pepper
Fresh herbs to serve

Melt the butter in a large frying pan. Add the garlic and vegetables and cook for a few minutes, stirring. Add the parsley. Whisk the eggs, season well with salt and pepper and pour over vegetables in the pan. Cook slowly, stir once or twice, then leave until eggs almost set. Put pan under a preheated grill to brown. Run a palette knife underneath to loosen the omelette, then slide out on to a serving dish, sprinkle with fresh herbs and serve at once.
Serves 4

Mushroom Risotto

Metric
1 onion, sliced
75g butter
225g brown rice
150ml dry white wine
600ml homemade stock
225g mushrooms, sliced
2 × 15ml spoons chopped
  fresh basil
Salt and pepper
2–3 × 15ml spoons Parmesan
  cheese, grated
To serve:
350g shelled prawns
50g garlic butter

Imperial
1 onion, sliced
3oz butter
$\frac{1}{2}$lb brown rice
$\frac{1}{4}$ pint dry white wine
1 pint homemade stock
$\frac{1}{2}$lb mushrooms, sliced
2tbsps chopped fresh basil
Salt and pepper
2–3tbsps Parmesan cheese,
  grated
To serve:
$\frac{3}{4}$lb shelled prawns
2oz garlic butter

Fry the onion in butter until golden, add the rice and cook for a further 10 minutes. Pour in the wine and allow to bubble briskly until well reduced. Add about a third of the stock, the mushrooms, basil and seasoning. Cook in an open pan over a moderate heat until the liquid has been absorbed. Gradually add the remaining stock and simmer until the rice is just soft, about 25–30 minutes. Turn into a hot serving dish, sprinkle with Parmesan cheese and serve at once with prawns which have been fried in garlic butter until hot.
Serves 4

Stuffed Peppers

Metric
4 large red peppers
4 × 15ml spoons peas
4 × 15ml spoons sweetcorn
  kernels
125g patna rice, cooked
225g chicken, cooked and
  diced
125g salami, diced
Salt and pepper
6 × 15ml spoons French
  dressing
1 clove garlic, crushed,
  optional
1 × 15ml spoon chopped onion

Imperial
4 large red peppers
4tbsps peas
4tbsps sweetcorn kernels
4oz patna rice, cooked
$\frac{1}{2}$lb chicken, cooked and diced
4oz salami, diced
Salt and pepper
6tbsps French dressing
1 clove garlic, crushed,
  optional
1tbsp chopped onion

Cut the tops off the peppers, scoop out seeds and core. Blanch for 2 minutes, drain and cool. Cook the peas and sweetcorn in boiling salted water for 5–7 minutes. Drain and cool. Combine peas and sweetcorn with the rice; stir in the remaining ingredients. Mix well and pile mixture into the peppers. Allow to stand for at least 1 hour to develop the flavour. Serve lightly chilled with a salad.
Serves 4

Vegetable Lasagne*

Metric	Imperial
10 sheets lasagne pasta	10 sheets lasagne pasta
4 × 15ml spoons oil	4tbsps oil
450g onions, sliced	1lb onions, sliced
450g tomatoes, skinned and sliced	1lb tomatoes, skinned and sliced
450g courgettes, sliced	1lb courgettes, sliced
2 cloves garlic, crushed	2 cloves garlic, crushed
1 × 5ml spoon dried basil	1tsp dried basil
150ml dry white wine	¼ pint dry white wine
Salt and pepper	Salt and pepper
50g butter	2oz butter
50g flour	2oz flour
600ml milk	1 pint milk
2 × 5ml spoons made mustard	2 teaspoons made mustard
175g strong Cheddar cheese, grated	6oz strong Cheddar cheese, grated

Cook the lasagne in boiling salted water with 3 × 15ml spoons (3tbsps) of the oil added to the water. Boil rapidly for 12–15 minutes until the pasta is just tender, drain and cool. Cook the onions, tomatoes and courgettes in the remaining oil, and add the garlic, basil, wine and seasoning. Bring to the boil, cover, and simmer gently for 25 minutes.

Meanwhile, melt the butter in a pan, add the flour and cook for 2 minutes. Gradually add the milk, stirring well, bring to the boil and cook for a further 2 minutes. Add salt, pepper and mustard, stir in the vegetables, and add most of the cheese, reserving a little for the top. Line an ovenproof dish with a third of the pasta, spoon over a third of the sauce, and continue layering, finishing with sauce. Sprinkle over the remaining cheese. Bake at 180°C/350°F, Gas Mark 4 for 25–30 minutes.

To freeze Freeze unbaked. Cover with foil and freeze.

To serve Thaw at room temperature for 6–7 hours then cook as above.

Serves 4

Herb Flan*

Metric	Imperial
Shortcrust pastry made with 175g flour and 75g fat	Shortcrust pastry made with 6oz flour and 3oz fat
25g butter	1oz butter
1 onion, chopped	1 onion, chopped
25g flour	1oz flour
300ml milk	½ pint milk
125g strong Cheddar cheese, grated	4oz strong Cheddar cheese, grated
Salt and pepper	Salt and pepper
2 × 15ml spoons chopped fresh herbs, e.g. basil and marjoram	2tbsps chopped fresh herbs, e.g. basil and marjoram
2 eggs, separated	2 eggs, separated
To garnish:	*To garnish:*
1 tomato, sliced	1 tomato, sliced
Fennel leaves	Fennel leaves

Use the pastry to line a 20cm (8in) flan ring. Bake blind, near the top of the oven, at 220°C/425°F, Gas Mark 7, for 15–20 minutes or until cooked but still pale in colour. Melt the butter and cook onion until transparent; stir in the flour and cook for 2–3 minutes. Gradually add the milk, stirring all the time. Bring to the boil and continue to stir until the sauce thickens. Remove from the heat and stir in the cheese, seasoning and herbs. Add the egg yolks and mix well. Whisk the egg whites until stiff and fold into the sauce. Pour into the pastry case and bake for a further 25–30 minutes until well risen and golden brown. Garnish with sliced tomato and fennel leaves. Serve hot or cold.

To freeze Open freeze and wrap in foil.

To serve Thaw at room temperature for 4–5 hours.

Serves 4–6

Haddock with Fennel and Celery Sauce*

Metric	Imperial
1kg fresh haddock	2lb fresh haddock
65g butter	2½oz butter
Salt and pepper	Salt and pepper
3 stalks celery, chopped	3 stalks celery, chopped
1 small head fennel, chopped	1 small head fennel, chopped
600ml milk	1 pint milk
50g flour	2oz flour
1 × 15ml spoon grated Parmesan cheese	1tbsp grated Parmesan cheese
1 lemon, sliced, to garnish	1 lemon, sliced, to garnish
Fennel leaves, to garnish	Fennel leaves, to garnish

Place the fish in a greased ovenproof dish, dot with 15g (½oz) butter and season with salt and pepper. Put the celery and fennel in a pan of boiling salted water and simmer for 15 minutes. Drain. Spoon the vegetables over the fish, pour over the milk, cover the dish with a lid or foil, and cook at 180°C/350°F, Gas Mark 4 for 12–15 minutes until the fish is just cooked. Drain the liquor from the fish, and reserve. Melt the remaining butter in a pan, stir in the flour and cook for 2 minutes. Gradually stir in the liquor, bring to the boil, and cook, stirring occasionally, for 3 minutes. Pour the sauce over the fish, sprinkle over the Parmesan cheese and return to the oven for about 20 minutes until heated through and bubbling. If the top is not really browned, put the dish under a hot grill for a few minutes. Serve hot, garnished with lemon and fennel.

To freeze Wrap in foil after sprinkling over the cheese, cool quickly and freeze.

To serve Thaw at room temperature for 7–8 hours. Bake for 30 minutes at 180°C/350°F, Gas Mark 4, brown under grill and garnish.

Serves 4

Prawn Stuffed Aubergines

Metric	Imperial
4 large aubergines	4 large aubergines
2 × 15ml spoons oil	2tbsps oil
3 medium onions, sliced	3 medium onions, sliced
450g tomatoes, skinned and sliced	1lb tomatoes, skinned and sliced
150ml dry white wine	¼ pint dry white wine
1 × 15ml spoon tomato purée	1tbsp tomato purée
1 clove garlic, crushed	1 clove garlic, crushed
Salt and pepper	Salt and pepper
225g shelled prawns	½lb shelled prawns

Halve the aubergines lengthways and scoop out the insides to within 6mm (¼in) of the skin. Blanch the shells for 4 minutes, and drain. Heat the oil in a pan, and gently cook the onions until golden brown; add the tomatoes. Chop up the pulp from the aubergines and add to the mixture. Add the wine, tomato purée, garlic and salt and pepper. Simmer, covered, for 25 minutes, then add the prawns. Arrange the aubergine shells in an ovenproof dish, spoon the prawn filling into each shell, cover with a lid or foil, and bake at 200°C/400°F, Gas Mark 6 for about 35–40 minutes or until tender and hot.
Serves 4

Onion and Cheese Bake

Metric	Imperial
12 slices bread	12 slices bread
Approx. 50g softened butter	Approx. 2oz softened butter
2 × 15ml spoons oil	2tbsps oil
3 medium onions, sliced	3 medium onions, sliced
½kg tomatoes, skinned and sliced	1lb tomatoes, skinned and sliced
225g Gruyère cheese, grated	½lb Gruyère cheese, grated
Mixed herbs	Mixed herbs
3 large eggs, beaten	3 large eggs, beaten
600ml milk	1 pint milk
Salt and pepper	Salt and pepper
225g streaky bacon rashers	½lb streaky bacon rashers

Trim the crusts from the bread, spread one side with butter. Use a few slices to line the base of a 1.1 litre (2 pint) ovenproof dish. Heat the oil in a pan, fry the onions until golden brown, cool slightly. Arrange a layer of onions and tomatoes on top of the bread, sprinkle with grated cheese and herbs, place another layer of buttered bread on top. Continue layering, finishing with bread, and top with cheese. Mix the eggs and milk together, season well with salt and pepper, pour over the bread layers. Bake at 180°C/350°F, Gas Mark 4 for 45 minutes to 1 hour, until well risen and golden brown. Roll the bacon rashers into rolls, secure with a cocktail stick. Fry or grill the bacon until cooked and crisp. Serve on top of the onion and cheese bake.
Serves 4

Bacon and Onion Roly Poly

Metric	Imperial
225g self-raising flour	½lb self-raising flour
1 × 5ml spoon baking powder	1tsp baking powder
1 × 2.5ml spoon salt	½tsp salt
100g suet	4oz suet
Water to mix	Water to mix
1 × 15ml spoon oil	1tbsp oil
3 medium onions, sliced	3 medium onions, sliced
4 rashers bacon, chopped	4 rashers bacon, chopped
175g strong Cheddar cheese, grated	6oz strong Cheddar cheese, grated
1 × 5ml spoon chopped fresh sage	1tsp chopped fresh sage
1 beaten egg, to glaze	1 beaten egg, to glaze

Sift the flour, baking powder and salt into a mixing bowl, stir in the suet and add sufficient water to make a fairly stiff dough. Roll into an oblong 30 × 15cm (12 × 6in) on a floured board. Heat the oil in a pan, and fry the onions and bacon until just cooked. Allow to cool and spoon over the pastry. Sprinkle the grated cheese over the onion mixture, and top with sage. Brush the sides of the pastry with beaten egg, roll up into an oblong and seal the ends. Make 4 diagonal cuts in the top of the pastry, put on a baking sheet and bake at 190°C/375°F, Gas Mark 5 for 1 hour or until golden brown.
Serves 4

Onion and Cheese Rarebits

Metric	Imperial
25g butter	1oz butter
225g strong Cheddar cheese, grated	½lb strong Cheddar cheese, grated
1 × 5ml spoon dry mustard	1tsp dry mustard
2 × 15ml spoons chopped chives	2tbsps chopped chives
Salt and pepper	Salt and pepper
3–4 × 15ml spoons brown ale	3–4tbsps brown ale
1 onion, chopped	1 onion, chopped
Freshly toasted bread	Freshly toasted bread
Garnish:	*Garnish:*
Radish roses	Radish roses
Spring onions	Spring onions

Melt the butter in a shallow saucepan, remove from the heat and stir in the cheese, mustard, chives, seasoning, brown ale and onion. Return to the heat and stir continuously until smooth and creamy, but do not allow to become more than just hot, otherwise the mixture will become stringy. Spread on the hot toast and put under a hot grill until golden and bubbling. Garnish with radish roses and spring onions. Serve at once.
Serves 4–6

Bacon and onion roly poly with onion and cheese rarebits

Salads

Tomato and Vegetable Ring

Metric
20g powdered unflavoured gelatine
900ml homemade stock
2 × 15ml spoons sherry
2 large tomatoes, skinned and sliced
½kg cooked and chopped mixed vegetables, e.g. fresh carrots, peas, beans, sweetcorn and celery
1 bunch watercress

Imperial
¾oz powdered unflavoured gelatine
1½ pints homemade stock
2tbsps sherry
2 large tomatoes, skinned and sliced
1lb cooked and chopped mixed vegetables, e.g. fresh carrots, peas, beans, sweetcorn and celery
1 bunch watercress

Put the gelatine in a basin with 2 × 15ml spoons (2tbsps) water and heat gently over a pan of hot water until melted. Stir into stock and add sherry. Pour 150ml (¼ pint) stock mixture into a 1 litre (2 pint) ring mould and allow to set. Arrange one tomato in the mould, spoon over sufficient stock to cover the slices; allow to set. Repeat the process with the other tomato. Add the mixed vegetables to the remaining stock and carefully pour into the mould. Set in the refrigerator. Dip the mould in hot water for 1–2 seconds, invert mould and turn out onto a serving plate. Fill centre of mould with watercress and serve.
Serves 6–8

Pickled Herrings with Red Cabbage Salad

Metric
4 large herrings
150ml cider vinegar
150ml water
1 bayleaf
6 peppercorns
2 cloves
Salt and pepper
225g red cabbage, thinly sliced
1 large eating apple, peeled, cored and diced
2 small onions, sliced
2 stalks celery, diced
Dressing:
1 × 15ml spoon Meaux mustard
150ml double cream
Fennel sprigs to garnish

Imperial
4 large herrings
¼ pint cider vinegar
¼ pint water
1 bayleaf
6 peppercorns
2 cloves
Salt and pepper
½lb red cabbage, thinly sliced
1 large eating apple, peeled, cored and diced
2 small onions, sliced
2 stalks celery, diced
Dressing:
1tbsp Meaux mustard
¼ pint double cream
Fennel sprigs to garnish

Roll herrings from head to tail and secure with a cocktail stick. Place in an ovenproof dish, pour over the cider vinegar and water, add the bayleaf, peppercorns and cloves and season with salt and pepper. Cover with foil or a lid and cook for 40 minutes at 180°C/350°F, Gas Mark 4. Allow to cool, remove herrings and drain well. Mix the cabbage, apple, onions and celery together in a bowl.

To make the dressing: mix the mustard and cream together, season with salt and pepper and stir into the salad ingredients. Pile on to a serving dish and arrange the herrings in a row on top. Garnish with fennel.
Serves 4

Danish Blue Cheese Salad

Metric
2 celeriac roots, peeled and grated
2 large ripe pears, peeled and chopped
Juice of ½ lemon
1 bunch spring onions, chopped
125g stoned dates, chopped
50g button mushrooms, sliced
Salt and pepper
50g Danish blue cheese, crumbled
150ml double cream
1 endive, separated into leaves
50g salami, sliced and made into cornets

Imperial
2 celeriac roots, peeled and grated
2 large ripe pears, peeled and chopped
Juice of ½ lemon
1 bunch spring onions, chopped
4oz stoned dates, chopped
2oz button mushrooms, sliced
Salt and pepper
2oz Danish blue cheese, crumbled
¼ pint double cream
1 endive, separated into leaves
2oz salami, sliced and made into cornets

Mix together the celeriac and pears in a bowl. Sprinkle with the lemon juice. Add the onions, dates and mushrooms and season with salt and pepper. Put the cheese into a basin, mix in the cream, and add to the celeriac mixture. Stir thoroughly. Place the endive leaves on a serving dish and pile salad on top; garnish with the salami cornets.
Serves 4

Pickled herrings with salads of red cabbage and Danish blue cheese

Grapefruit and Grape Salad

Metric	Imperial
4 large grapefruit	4 large grapefruit
125g green grapes	4oz green grapes
50g Brazil nuts, roughly chopped	2oz Brazil nuts, roughly chopped
Dressing:	Dressing:
4 × 15ml spoons wine vinegar	4tbsps wine vinegar
6 × 15ml spoons olive oil	6tbsps olive oil
2 × 5ml spoons sugar	2tsps sugar
1 × 5ml spoon dry mustard	1tsp dry mustard
1 × 5ml spoon salt	1tsp salt
3 × 15ml spoons single cream	3tbsps single cream
Mustard and cress	Mustard and cress

Remove skin and pith from the grapefruit. Cut the fruit into segments and put into a bowl. Cut the grapes in half and remove the pips, add these and the nuts to the grapefruit. Put the dressing ingredients in a basin and mix thoroughly. Place the fruit and nuts on a serving dish, spoon dressing over them and garnish with mustard and cress.

Serves 4

Rice and Prawn Medley

Metric	Imperial
125g long grain rice	4oz long grain rice
75g sweetcorn	3oz sweetcorn
125g mushrooms, sliced	4oz mushrooms, sliced
125g green beans, cooked	4oz green beans, cooked
1 small onion, sliced	1 small onion, sliced
125g shelled prawns	4oz shelled prawns
3 small courgettes, sliced	3 small courgettes, sliced
25g butter	1oz butter
Salt and pepper	Salt and pepper
French dressing	French dressing
4 whole prawns with shells	4 whole prawns with shells

Cook the rice in boiling salted water for 12 minutes until just tender. Drain. Put the sweetcorn, mushrooms, beans, onion and peeled prawns in a bowl, add the rice and stir well. Fry the courgettes in butter until lightly coloured, drain on absorbent paper and add to the salad when cool. Season with salt and pepper, toss in French dressing, pile into a serving dish, and garnish with the whole prawns.

Serves 4

Waldorf Salad

Metric	Imperial
450g eating apples	1lb eating apples
Juice of 1 lemon	Juice of 1 lemon
150ml mayonnaise	$\frac{1}{4}$ pint mayonnaise
$\frac{1}{2}$ head celery, chopped	$\frac{1}{2}$ head celery, chopped
15g hazelnuts, chopped	$\frac{1}{2}$oz hazelnuts, chopped
15g walnuts, chopped	$\frac{1}{2}$oz walnuts, chopped
Salt and pepper	Salt and pepper
1 lettuce	1 lettuce
1 × 15ml spoon snipped chives	1tbsp snipped chives

Peel and core the apples, slice one and dice the rest; dip the slices in lemon juice to prevent discoloration. Toss diced apples in the mayonnaise, stir in the celery, hazelnuts and walnuts and season with salt and pepper. Arrange the lettuce on a dish and pile the salad in the centre. Arrange the apple slices on top and sprinkle over with chives.

Serves 4

Curried Chicken Salad

Metric	Imperial
350g cooked chicken	$\frac{3}{4}$lb cooked chicken
1 × 15ml spoon curry powder	1tbsp curry powder
1 clove garlic, crushed	1 clove garlic, crushed
150ml mayonnaise	$\frac{1}{4}$ pint mayonnaise
150ml soured cream	$\frac{1}{4}$ pint soured cream
1 green pepper, seeded and chopped	1 green pepper, seeded and chopped
1 egg, hard-boiled and chopped	1 egg, hard-boiled and chopped
1 × 15ml spoon tomato purée	1tbsp tomato purée
125g mushrooms, sliced	4oz mushrooms, sliced
Salt and pepper	Salt and pepper
Endive	Endive
225g asparagus, cooked	$\frac{1}{2}$lb asparagus, cooked
2 tomatoes, quartered	2 tomatoes, quartered

Cut the chicken into chunks. Put the curry powder in a bowl, add the garlic, mayonnaise and soured cream. Mix well and allow to stand for $\frac{1}{2}$ hour. Stir in the green pepper, hard-boiled egg, tomato purée and mushrooms and season with salt and pepper. Mix in the chicken. Arrange the endive on a dish, pile the chicken salad on top and garnish with asparagus and tomatoes.

Serves 4

Waldorf salad with grapefruit and grape salad

Caesar Salad

Metric	Imperial
225g chicory	½lb chicory
½ small cucumber, sliced	½ small cucumber, sliced
6 radishes, cut into roses	6 radishes, cut into roses
3 slices bread, cubed	3 slices bread, cubed
1 egg, beaten	1 egg, beaten
25g Parmesan cheese, grated	1oz Parmesan cheese, grated
1 × 5ml spoon dry mustard	1tsp dry mustard
1 × 15ml spoon oil	1tbsp oil
25g butter	1oz butter
1 clove garlic, crushed	1 clove garlic, crushed

Arrange the chicory, cucumber and radish roses around the edge of a serving dish. Coat the bread cubes in beaten egg. Mix the Parmesan cheese and dry mustard together and toss the bread cubes in the mixture. Heat the oil and butter in a frying pan. Lightly fry the garlic, then fry the bread cubes until golden brown and crisp. Cool. Pile in the centre of the chicory border and serve at once.
Serves 4

Winter Salad

Metric	Imperial
3 apples, cored and sliced	3 apples, cored and sliced
4 stalks celery, chopped	4 stalks celery, chopped
1 onion, sliced	1 onion, sliced
1 medium beetroot, cooked, peeled and diced	1 medium beetroot, cooked, peeled and diced
Approx. 150ml mayonnaise	Approx. ¼ pint mayonnaise
Salt and pepper	Salt and pepper
1 lettuce	1 lettuce
25g walnuts, chopped	1oz walnuts, chopped
1 × 15ml spoon chopped parsley	1tbsp chopped parsley

Mix the apples, celery, onion and beetroot together, add sufficient mayonnaise to coat, and season well with salt and pepper. Pile on to a bed of lettuce leaves, sprinkle over with walnuts and chopped parsley and serve.
Serves 4

French Bean and Orange Salad

Metric	Imperial
450g French beans	1lb French beans
3 oranges	3 oranges
½ cucumber	½ cucumber
Dressing:	*Dressing:*
150ml mayonnaise	¼ pint mayonnaise
1 × 15ml spoon chopped stuffed olives	1tbsp chopped stuffed olives
1 × 15ml spoon chopped onion	1tbsp chopped onion
1 egg, hard-boiled	1 egg, hard-boiled
1 × 15ml spoon chopped green pepper	1tbsp chopped green pepper
1 × 5ml spoon chopped parsley	1tsp chopped parsley
1 × 5ml spoon tomato purée	1tsp tomato purée

Cook the beans in boiling salted water for 5–7 minutes, until just tender. Remove skin and pith from the oranges and cut into segments. Pile the beans in the centre of a flat dish and arrange the orange segments and sliced cucumber, overlapping each other, round the edge of the beans. Mix all the dressing ingredients together and spoon over the salad just before serving.
Serves 4–6

Christmas Salad

Metric	Imperial
225–350g broad beans, cooked	½–¾lb broad beans, cooked
350g small Brussels sprouts	¾lb small Brussels sprouts
3 stalks celery	3 stalks celery
1 medium onion, chopped	1 medium onion, chopped
50g sultanas	2oz sultanas
50g seedless raisins	2oz seedless raisins
2 grapefruit, or frozen sections	2 grapefruit, or frozen sections
4–5 × 15ml spoons French dressing	4–5tbsps French dressing
1 × 5ml spoon French mustard	1tsp French mustard
25g salted peanuts	1oz salted peanuts
1–2 small tomatoes	1–2 small tomatoes
1 small carrot	1 small carrot

Mix prepared beans and sprouts. Cut celery into 5cm (2in) lengths and then into thin strips. Drop about one-third into iced water to curl and add rest to the beans with the onion. Mix sultanas, raisins and grapefruit sections and add 2 × 15ml spoons (2tbsps) French dressing. Add mustard to remaining dressing and pour over raw vegetables. Chill. Just before serving fold the two mixtures together and spoon on to a serving platter. Sprinkle nuts on top and decorate with tomatoes cut into sections, grated carrot and the curled celery. If liked, bite-sized pieces of turkey, duck, or other cold meats can be folded into the vegetables.
Serves 4

Caesar salad and French bean and orange salad

Red and Green Salad

Metric
2 bunches watercress, roughly
  chopped
12 spring onions, sliced
1 small red pepper, seeded and
  sliced
10cm piece cucumber, halved
  and thinly sliced
Approx. 2 × 15ml spoons
  French dressing
6–8 small tomatoes

Imperial
2 bunches watercress, roughly
  chopped
12 spring onions, sliced
1 small red pepper, seeded and
  sliced
4in piece cucumber, halved
  and thinly sliced
Approx. 2tbsps French
  dressing
6–8 small tomatoes

Mix the watercress, onions, red pepper and cucumber together, add the French dressing and toss lightly. Put into a dish. Cut each tomato into 6–8 sections and use, with the skin side uppermost, to decorate the top of the salad.
Serves 6

Italian Pasta Salad

Metric
175g pasta shells
225g streaky bacon, chopped
175g continental smoked garlic
  sausage, cut diagonally into
  1cm pieces
175g black grapes, halved and
  pipped
125g red pepper, seeded and
  sliced
Dressing:
125g plain yogurt
125g double cream
1 × 15ml spoon chopped fresh
  mint
2 × 5ml spoons lemon juice
Salt and pepper

Imperial
6oz pasta shells
½lb streaky bacon, chopped
6oz continental smoked garlic
  sausage, cut diagonally into
  ½in pieces
6oz black grapes, halved and
  pipped
4oz red pepper, seeded and
  sliced
Dressing:
4oz plain yogurt
4oz double cream
1tbsp chopped fresh mint
2tsps lemon juice
Salt and pepper

Cook the pasta in boiling salted water for 9–12 minutes until just tender. Drain. Fry the bacon in its own fat until crispy; drain well. Put the pasta, bacon, garlic sausage, grapes and red pepper in a bowl and mix well.

To make the dressing: put the yogurt, double cream, mint, lemon juice and salt and pepper in a bowl and mix well. Pour over the pasta salad and stir. Pile into a serving dish and allow to stand for ½ hour before serving.
Serves 4

Raw Mushroom and Spinach Salad

Metric
125g small, very fresh
  mushrooms, thinly sliced
French dressing
125g spinach, washed and
  drained

Imperial
4oz small, very fresh
  mushrooms, thinly sliced
French dressing
4oz spinach, washed and
  drained

Put the mushrooms into a lidded container with 2 × 15ml spoons (2tbsps) French dressing. Shake to coat evenly and refrigerate for at least 2 hours; shake gently from time to time. Just before serving remove thick centre stalks from spinach, slice the green leaves finely and mix with the mushrooms, adding more dressing if required to coat the spinach.
Serves 4

Hot Potato Salad

Metric
1 large onion, chopped
4 × 15ml spoons oil
2 × 5ml spoons flour
2 × 5ml spoons sugar
Salt and pepper
150ml tarragon vinegar
150ml chicken stock
½kg potatoes, cooked and
  sliced
4 spring onions, chopped
½ green pepper, seeded and
  chopped
4 dill pickles, chopped
1 × 15ml spoon chopped
  parsley

Imperial
1 large onion, chopped
4tbsps oil
2tsps flour
2tsps sugar
Salt and pepper
¼ pint tarragon vinegar
¼ pint chicken stock
2lb potatoes, cooked and
  sliced
4 spring onions, chopped
½ green pepper, seeded and
  chopped
4 dill pickles, chopped
1tbsp chopped parsley

Fry the onion in the oil until tender but not coloured, stir in the flour and cook for 1 minute. Add the sugar and salt and pepper and gradually stir in the vinegar and stock. Bring to the boil, stirring, and cook for 2 minutes. Stir in the sliced potatoes, spring onions, pepper and pickles. The vegetables should be well coated and heated through. Just before serving sprinkle with the chopped parsley.
Serves 4–6

Salade Niçoise

Metric
450g tomatoes, skinned and sliced
½ cucumber, sliced
Salt and pepper
1 × 5ml spoon chopped parsley
1 × 5ml spoon chopped fresh basil
125g French beans, cooked
225g can tuna fish, drained
½ green pepper, seeded and chopped
50g black olives, pitted and chopped
1 clove garlic, crushed
French dressing
2 eggs, hard-boiled and quartered
8 anchovy fillets
1 lemon, quartered

Imperial
1lb tomatoes, skinned and sliced
½ cucumber, sliced
Salt and pepper
1tsp chopped parsley
1tsp chopped fresh basil
4oz French beans, cooked
½lb can tuna fish, drained
½ green pepper, seeded and chopped
2oz black olives, pitted and chopped
1 clove garlic, crushed
French dressing
2 eggs, hard-boiled and quartered
8 anchovy fillets
1 lemon, quartered

Arrange the tomatoes in layers with the cucumber on a shallow dish. Season with salt and pepper and sprinkle over with herbs. Mix the beans, tuna and pepper together and pile in the centre of the dish; sprinkle with the black olives. Add the garlic to the dressing, and pour over the salad. Arrange the eggs and anchovy fillets attractively on top and garnish with lemon. Allow the salad to stand for about ½ hour before serving to allow the flavours to blend.
Serves 4–6

Strawberry and Walnut Salad

Metric
225g asparagus, cooked
450g strawberries, sliced
50g walnuts, cut into halves
10cm piece cucumber, sliced
Dressing:
2 egg yolks
Salt and pepper
150ml olive oil
2 × 15ml spoons lemon juice
1 egg white, stiffly whisked

Imperial
½lb asparagus, cooked
1lb strawberries, sliced
2oz walnuts, cut into halves
4in piece cucumber, sliced
Dressing:
2 egg yolks
Salt and pepper
¼ pint olive oil
2tbsps lemon juice
1 egg white, stiffly whisked

Arrange the asparagus in a circle on a serving platter, to resemble the sun's rays, i.e. pointed ends towards the edge of the dish. Mix the strawberries with the walnuts and cucumber.

To make the dressing: cream the egg yolks and seasoning together. Add the oil drop by drop, stirring all the time until the mayonnaise is thick. Stir in the lemon juice. Just before serving fold in the whisked egg white.

Arrange the strawberry mixture in the centre of the dish and spoon over some of the dressing. Serve the remaining dressing separately.
Serves 4–6

Coleslaw

Metric
½ white cabbage, shredded
4 stalks celery, chopped
1 medium onion, chopped
4 large carrots, grated
Salt and pepper
4 × 15ml spoons mayonnaise
Few drops lemon juice
Variations:
1. ¼ small raw cauliflower, sliced
   2 red-skinned apples, cored and chopped
   25g walnuts, chopped
2. 25–50g sultanas
   25–50g raisins
   1 × 15ml spoon chopped parsley
   2 × 15ml spoons salted peanuts
3. 2 oranges, peeled and cut into segments
   12 dates, stoned and chopped
   50g cobnuts, chopped

Imperial
½ white cabbage, shredded
4 stalks celery, chopped
1 medium onion, chopped
4 large carrots, grated
Salt and pepper
4tbsps mayonnaise
Few drops lemon juice
Variations:
1. ¼ small raw cauliflower, sliced
   2 red-skinned apples, cored and chopped
   1oz walnuts, chopped
2. 1–2oz sultanas
   1–2oz raisins
   1tbsp chopped parsley
   2tbsps salted peanuts
3. 2 oranges, peeled and cut into segments
   12 dates, stoned and chopped
   2oz cobnuts, chopped

Combine the cabbage, celery and onion together in a large bowl. Stir in the carrots and seasoning. Stir in the mayonnaise and lemon juice making sure all the vegetables are well coated. The salad can be left up to an hour before serving, covered and in a cool place, to absorb the flavour of the dressing. If liked, add any of the three variations. Chopped apple, however, should only be added immediately before serving.
Serves 6–8

Vegetable Side Dishes

Herb and Potato Dumplings

Metric
1½kg potatoes, peeled
2 × 5ml spoons baking powder
1 × 5ml spoon salt
1 × 2.5ml spoon grated nutmeg
50g semolina
75g wheatmeal flour
2 eggs, beaten
2 × 15ml spoons chopped
  fresh mixed herbs: parsley,
  thyme, sage, marjoram
1 small onion, grated
2 slices bread
Oil
125g bacon, chopped

Imperial
3lb potatoes, peeled
2tsps baking powder
1tsp salt
½tsp grated nutmeg
2oz semolina
3oz wheatmeal flour
2 eggs, beaten
2tbsps chopped fresh mixed
  herbs: parsley, thyme, sage,
  marjoram
1 small onion, grated
2 slices bread
Oil
4oz bacon, chopped

Cook the potatoes, sieve and cool. Add the baking powder, salt, nutmeg, semolina, flour, eggs, herbs and onion. Knead to a smooth dough. Remove the crusts from the bread and cut it into cubes. Heat the oil and fry the bread cubes until crisp and golden brown. Flour the hands and make the dough into round dumplings, about the size of a fist. Press a few of the fried croûtons into each dumpling. Put the dumplings into boiling salted water and cook thoroughly for 12–15 minutes. Lightly fry the bacon. Put the dumplings in a serving dish and sprinkle with the bacon pieces. Serve with boiled ham or a pot roast.
Serves 4–6

Brussels Sprouts with Chestnuts

Metric
350g chestnuts
600ml homemade stock
1 stalk celery
1 small onion
1 × 5ml spoon sugar
1 bouquet garni
¾kg Brussels sprouts
50g butter

Imperial
¾lb chestnuts
1 pint homemade stock
1 stalk celery
1 small onion
1tsp sugar
1 bouquet garni
1½lb Brussels sprouts
2oz butter

Put the chestnuts in a pan of cold water and bring to the boil. Drain. Remove both the outside and inside skins. Put the nuts in a pan, cover with the stock and add the celery, onion, sugar and bouquet garni. Bring to the boil, cover, and simmer until the nuts are soft, about 35–40 minutes. Drain, removing the celery, onion and bouquet garni; keep the chestnuts hot. Meanwhile prepare the Brussels sprouts: trim off outer leaves and cut a cross at the base of each stalk. Cook the sprouts in boiling salted water for 10–12 minutes until just soft. Drain, return to the pan, add the chestnuts and butter and toss. Serve hot.
Serves 4–6

Mexican Style Corn

Metric
1 onion, chopped
1 carrot, peeled and cubed
1 stalk celery, chopped
350g sweetcorn kernels, fresh
  or frozen
1 green pepper, seeded and
  sliced
1 red pepper, seeded and
  sliced
1 bayleaf
25g butter
25g flour
150ml milk
Salt and pepper
1 × 5ml spoon chopped fresh
  basil

Imperial
1 onion, chopped
1 carrot, peeled and cubed
1 stalk celery, chopped
¾lb sweetcorn kernels, fresh or
  frozen
1 green pepper, seeded and
  sliced
1 red pepper, seeded and
  sliced
1 bayleaf
1oz butter
1oz flour
¼ pint milk
Salt and pepper
1tsp chopped fresh basil

Put the vegetables in a pan, add the bayleaf, cover with water and bring to the boil. Cover and simmer for 15 minutes. Drain well, but reserve 150ml (¼ pint) water from the vegetables. Melt the butter in a pan, stir in the flour and cook for 2 minutes. Gradually add the vegetable water and the milk, stirring all the time. Bring to the boil, and cook for 2 minutes. Adjust seasoning to taste, stir in the vegetables, pour into a serving dish and serve hot, sprinkled with chopped basil.
Serves 4

Herb and potato dumplings served with ham

Northumberland Pan Haggerty

Metric	Imperial
25–50g dripping	1–2oz dripping
1kg potatoes, peeled and thinly sliced	2lb potatoes, peeled and thinly sliced
½kg onions, thinly sliced	1lb onions, thinly sliced
2 × 15ml spoons chopped parsley	2tbsps chopped parsley
125g Cheddar cheese, grated	4oz Cheddar cheese, grated
Salt and pepper	Salt and pepper

Heat the dripping in a large heavy frying pan and put in the potatoes and onions in alternate layers, separating each layer with a sprinkling of parsley, grated cheese and seasoning. Fry gently until browned, turn over and brown the other side. Cover pan and cook until potatoes are tender.
Serves 4

Pommes Lyonnaise

Metric	Imperial
¾kg potatoes	1½lb potatoes
2 × 15ml spoons oil	2tbsps oil
25g butter	1oz butter
2 large onions, sliced	2 large onions, sliced
Salt and pepper	Salt and pepper
1 × 15ml spoon chopped parsley	1tbsp chopped parsley

Scrub the potatoes and boil them in their skins until nearly tender. Drain, remove the skins and slice. Heat the oil and butter in a heavy based frying pan; fry the potatoes and onions until golden brown and the potatoes crisp. Remove from the heat, sprinkle over the salt and pepper and parsley. Turn into a serving dish and serve at once.
Serves 4

Vegetable Dumplings

Metric	Imperial
100g self-raising flour	4oz self-raising flour
1 × 2.5ml spoon baking powder	½tsp baking powder
50g shredded suet	2oz shredded suet
1 × 2.5ml spoon salt	½tsp salt
1 small carrot, peeled and grated	1 small carrot, peeled and grated
2 × 15ml spoons chopped parsley	2tbsps chopped parsley
Water to mix	Water to mix

Cook and serve with roast meat.
Sift the flour and baking powder into a mixing bowl; stir in the suet and salt. Add the carrot and parsley, and mix in sufficient water to make a stiff dough. Be careful not to add too much water. Flour your hands and form the mixture into small dumplings, about the size of a walnut. Place in a roasting tin round the joint of meat, and cook, turning once, for 15–20 minutes, until well risen and thoroughly cooked, at 180°C/350°F, Gas Mark 4. Serve at once.
Serves 4

Savoury Pumpkin

Metric	Imperial
2 × 15ml spoons oil	2 tbsps oil
1 large onion, sliced	1 large onion, sliced
4 large tomatoes, skinned and sliced	4 large tomatoes, skinned and sliced
225–275g pumpkin, skinned, seeded and sliced	8–10oz pumpkin, skinned, seeded and sliced
1 × 5ml spoon dried basil	1tsp dried basil
Salt and pepper	Salt and pepper

Heat the oil in a pan, add the onion, and cook for 5 minutes. Arrange the tomatoes on top of the onions, and top with the pumpkin. Sprinkle basil between each layer, and season well. Cover and simmer gently for 30 minutes. Serve hot with roast and grilled meats.
Serves 4

Beetroot with Soured Cream and Chives

Metric	Imperial
450g cooked beetroot, peeled and diced	1lb cooked beetroot, peeled and diced
25g butter	1oz butter
Salt and freshly ground black pepper	Salt and freshly ground black pepper
5 × 15ml spoons soured cream	5tbsps soured cream
1–2 × 15ml spoons chopped chives	1–2tbsps chopped chives

Put the beetroot and butter into a pan and heat gently until thoroughly hot. Season with salt and pepper. Push to one side of the pan, pour soured cream into the other and heat. Then mix the two together, sprinkle with the chives and serve at once.
   If fresh chives are not available, chive butter can be used.
Serves 4–6

Northumberland pan haggerty with savoury pumpkin

Colcannon or Bubble and Squeak

Metric
½kg cooked potatoes
150–450g cooked cabbage
Salt and freshly ground black
  pepper
50g bacon fat, butter or good
  dripping
Chopped parsley

Imperial
1lb cooked potatoes
5oz–1lb cooked cabbage
Salt and freshly ground black
  pepper
2oz bacon fat, butter or good
  dripping
Chopped parsley

An old recipe which has long been popular just because it is so good, try varying the proportions until you find the one you like best.
Mash the potatoes, chop the cabbage and mix the two together with salt and pepper. Melt the fat in a frying pan, put in the vegetables and form into a large cake about 2.5cm (1in) thick. Cook fairly slowly until the underside is well-browned; cut into half and turn each half carefully. Heat and brown the second side.

Or, if the oven is in use cook the colcannon in it. Melt the fat in the frying pan, add vegetables, heat and stir until the vegetables are hot. Transfer to a greased pie dish or casserole so the cake is about 2.5cm (1in) thick, and bake in a hot oven, 200°C/400°F, Gas Mark 6, for about ½ hour.

Brussels sprouts or kale can replace all or part of the cabbage.
Serves 4–6

Young Turnips and Mushrooms

Metric
450g young turnips, peeled
50g butter or herb butter,
  e.g. thyme
1 rasher back bacon, chopped
125g mushrooms, trimmed,
  wiped and sliced
Salt and freshly ground black
  pepper

Imperial
1lb young turnips, peeled
2oz butter or herb butter,
  e.g. thyme
1 rasher back bacon, chopped
4oz mushrooms, trimmed,
  wiped and sliced
Salt and freshly ground black
  pepper

You need really young turnips for this dish which is good enough to serve as a separate vegetable course before the main dish.
Cut the prepared turnips into 6mm (¼in) thick slices and boil in salted water for 10 minutes. Drain and keep hot. Meanwhile, melt 40g (1½oz) of the butter and fry the bacon and mushrooms for about 5 minutes. Season. Add the turnip, cover with a lid, and cook gently 5–10 minutes. Lift out turnip slices, arrange on a heated dish, and pour over the mushrooms and bacon. Serve hot with the remaining butter on top.
Serves 4–6

Peas with Mushrooms

Metric
Peas, fresh or frozen for 4
  people
1–2 sprigs fresh rosemary
1 × 5ml spoon sugar
25g butter
Very small onion, chopped
125g mushrooms, sliced
Salt and freshly ground black
  pepper
3 × 15ml spoons single cream

Imperial
Peas, fresh or frozen for 4
  people
1–2 sprigs fresh rosemary
1tsp sugar
1oz butter
Very small onion, chopped
4oz mushrooms, sliced
Salt and freshly ground black
  pepper
3tbsps single cream

Cook the peas in boiling salted water, with the rosemary, until soft. Drain and sprinkle with the sugar. Meanwhile, melt the butter, cook the onion until soft, add mushrooms and seasoning and cook until the mushrooms are tender. Mix with the peas, put into a heated serving dish and trickle the cream over.
Serves 4

Braised Fennel

Metric
4 small or 2 large bulbous
  stems Florentine fennel
Boiling chicken stock
25g butter
Salt and freshly ground black
  pepper

Imperial
4 small or 2 large bulbous
  stems Florentine fennel
Boiling chicken stock
1oz butter
Salt and freshly ground black
  pepper

Fennel has a strong flavour and goes well with roast meat.
Cut the fennel into halves downwards and wash well. Put into boiling stock to cover, and simmer about 10 minutes. Drain. Put into a casserole, put pats of butter on top, season, cover with a lid and put into the oven underneath the roast for 20–30 minutes, according to size.
Serves 4

Roast lamb with turnips and mushrooms and braised fennel

Red Cabbage Allemande*

Metric
Approx. ½kg red cabbage, trimmed and sliced
1 × 15ml spoon sugar
1 × 5ml spoon salt
2 × 15ml spoons red wine vinegar
25g butter
1 large onion, sliced
1 medium cooking apple, peeled, cored and sliced
300ml beef stock
4 crushed juniper berries
Freshly ground black pepper
1–2 × 15ml spoons redcurrant jelly

Imperial
Approx. 1lb red cabbage, trimmed and sliced
1tbsp sugar
1tsp salt
2tbsps red wine vinegar
1oz butter
1 large onion, sliced
1 medium cooking apple, peeled, cored and sliced
½ pint beef stock
4 crushed juniper berries
Freshly ground black pepper
1–2tbsps redcurrant jelly

This is very good served with the more fatty meats and poultry such as pork, duck and goose.
Put the prepared red cabbage into a large basin. Mix the sugar, salt and vinegar and when sugar and salt are dissolved pour over the cabbage and toss to coat evenly. Leave about ½ hour. Melt the butter, add the onion and apple and toss together until the butter is absorbed. Add the cabbage, beef stock and juniper berries, bring to the boil, cover and simmer for 45 minutes. Remove lid and cook a further 15 minutes or until the cabbage is tender and most of the liquid has evaporated. Add pepper and the redcurrant jelly to taste. Heat and stir until the jelly has dissolved.
To freeze After the 45 minute simmering, cool quickly, transfer to containers, seal, label and freeze.
To serve Put frozen block into a strong pan over low heat, with the lid on until thawed. Then heat in an uncovered pan to evaporate the liquid, and proceed as above.
Serves 4

Carrot Ring

Metric
¾kg carrots, peeled and chopped
3 eggs, separated
Good pinch dry mustard
1 × 15ml spoon grated onion
1 × 5ml spoon paprika
Salt and freshly ground black pepper
50g fresh white breadcrumbs

Imperial
1½lb carrots, peeled and chopped
3 eggs, separated
Good pinch dry mustard
1tbsp grated onion
1tsp paprika
Salt and freshly ground black pepper
2oz fresh white breadcrumbs

Cook the carrots in boiling salted water until tender. Drain and mash. Work in the egg yolks, one at a time, mustard, onion, paprika, seasoning and breadcrumbs. Whisk the egg whites until very stiff and dry and fold into the carrots. Grease a 1.1–1.4 litre (2–2½ pint) ring mould and put a strip of paper in the bottom to help turning out. Put the carrot mixture into the ring mould and stand in a tin of hot water. Cover all with aluminium foil and bake for 30 minutes at 190°C/375°F, Gas Mark 5. Turn out on to a heated dish.
To serve Fill the centre of the ring with some green vegetable such as broccoli, whole or sliced beans, peas, leeks or tiny, cooked mushrooms and onions. *Or*, add chopped poultry or shellfish to mushroom sauce and use to fill the centre.
Serves 4

Chinese Cabbage with Onions and Tomatoes

Metric
1 medium head Chinese cabbage, washed and quartered
50g butter
150ml chicken stock
Salt and freshly ground black pepper
1 medium onion, thinly sliced
1 clove garlic, crushed
125g tomatoes, skinned, seeded and chopped
1 × 5ml spoon mixed dried herbs

Imperial
1 medium head Chinese cabbage, washed and quartered
2oz butter
¼ pint chicken stock
Salt and freshly ground black pepper
1 medium onion, thinly sliced
1 clove garlic, crushed
4oz tomatoes, skinned, seeded and chopped
1tsp mixed dried herbs

This popular vegetable is cooked in the same way as cabbage but it does not have the strong smell often associated with boiled cabbage.
Put the quartered cabbage into boiling, salted water, boil 5 minutes and drain well. Melt 25g (1oz) butter in a pan just big enough to take the cabbage quarters in one layer. Put in the cabbage, stock and seasoning, cover and cook slowly until the cabbage is cooked (10–15 minutes). Meanwhile, melt remaining butter in a pan, add the onion and cook slowly until soft. Add the garlic, tomatoes, herbs and seasoning and cook a further 5 minutes. Strain liquid from cabbage into the tomato mixture and boil rapidly until tomato mixture is a thickish sauce. Put cabbage into a heated dish and pour tomato mixture on top.
Serves 4

Peas Bonne Femme

Metric	Imperial
3–4 rashers streaky bacon, rinded and chopped	3–4 rashers streaky bacon, rinded and chopped
18–24 small white onions, peeled	18–24 small white onions, peeled
1 × 15ml spoon flour	1tbsp flour
450ml chicken stock	¾ pint chicken stock
Salt and pepper	Salt and pepper
Peas, fresh or frozen, for 4 people	Peas, fresh or frozen, for 4 people
1 × 15ml spoon melted butter	1tbsp melted butter
Chopped parsley	Chopped parsley

Peas are one of our most popular vegetables and freeze very well, so this dish can be served at any time.

Put the prepared bacon into a dry, hot frying pan and, as the fat begins to run, put in the onions and fry carefully until they are golden brown. Lift out bacon and onions with a slotted spoon and pour out any fat in excess of 1 × 15ml spoon (1tbsp). Mix flour into retained fat and cook a few minutes. Add stock and seasoning. Heat and stir to make a smooth sauce; simmer 5 minutes. Add bacon and onions and cook a further 5 minutes (if using frozen peas extend this time to 10 minutes). Add peas and cook until tender. Just before serving, stir in the butter, put into a hot serving dish and sprinkle with chopped parsley.

Serves 4

French Beans with Egg and Lemon Sauce

Metric	Imperial
½kg small whole French beans, fresh or frozen	1lb small whole French beans, fresh or frozen
25g butter	1oz butter
25g flour	1oz flour
300ml chicken stock	½ pint chicken stock
Salt and pepper	Salt and pepper
2 eggs	2 eggs
Juice of 1 large or 2 smaller lemons	Juice of 1 large or 2 smaller lemons

This is a delicious way of serving tiny French beans and it looks very attractive. Try it with fish or chicken.

Cook the beans in boiling salted water until tender. Drain and put on to a heated flattish dish. Keep hot. Melt the butter and stir in the flour. Cook for 1 minute, then stir in the stock and seasoning. Bring to the boil and simmer, stirring, until thick and smooth. Beat the eggs until light and frothy, beat in the lemon juice and then stir in 3 tbsps of the sauce, one at a time. Return to pan, heat and stir to cook eggs, but do not boil. Test to see if enough lemon has been added and pour the sauce in a long stripe over the centre of the beans.

Serves 4

Asparagus Polonaise

Metric	Imperial
Asparagus, fresh or frozen, for 4 people	Asparagus, fresh or frozen, for 4 people
40g butter	1½oz butter
50g fresh white breadcrumbs	2oz fresh white breadcrumbs
Salt and pepper	Salt and pepper
2 hard-boiled eggs, chopped	2 hard-boiled eggs, chopped

Polonaise is a popular way of finishing many vegetables. Try this topping with Brussels sprouts, cauliflower, leeks or new potatoes as well.

Cook the asparagus carefully in boiling salted water until tender. Ideally this should be done with the asparagus in a special cage which holds the stalks upright with the green tops out of the water. Drain and arrange on a heated dish. Meanwhile, melt the butter, add the breadcrumbs and fry, carefully, until crisp and golden. Stir in the eggs and seasoning and heat through, then sprinkle over the asparagus.

Serves 4

Creamed Spinach

Metric	Imperial
½kg spinach	1lb spinach
5 × 15ml spoons soured cream	5tbsps soured cream
2 × 15ml spoons melted butter	2tbsps melted butter
1–2 × 15ml spoons grated horseradish	1–2tbsps grated horseradish
Salt and pepper	Salt and pepper
1 × 2.5ml spoon chopped fresh tarragon	½tsp chopped fresh tarragon

Weigh the spinach with the centre stalk removed. Wash it and put into a pan with the water clinging to its leaves, cover and cook 5–10 minutes until soft. Drain well, pressing out as much moisture as possible, and chop. Return to the pan with remaining ingredients and heat while stirring. Serve in a heated dish and, if liked, put a little soured cream on as a decoration or scatter with fried croûtons.

Frozen spinach can also be used.

Serves 4

French beans with egg and lemon sauce accompany a roast chicken

Kohlrabi in Butter

Metric	Imperial
½kg kohlrabi, peeled and thinly sliced	1lb kohlrabi, peeled and thinly sliced
50g butter	2oz butter
2 × 15ml spoons water	2tbsps water
Salt and pepper	Salt and pepper
Chopped parsley	Chopped parsley

Kohlrabi has a delicate turnip flavour and is best used when young and small.

Put the kohlrabi slices into a pan with the butter, water and seasoning. Bring to the boil, cover with the lid and cook slowly for about 10 minutes until almost tender. Remove the lid and cook a further 5 minutes to evaporate any remaining water. Transfer to a heated dish and sprinkle with the parsley.
Serves 4

Cabbage with Gruyère Cheese

Metric	Imperial
¾–1kg white or savoy cabbage, quartered	1½–2lb white or savoy cabbage, quartered
Bechamel sauce:	*Bechamel sauce:*
300ml milk	½ pint milk
½ small onion	½ small onion
6 white peppercorns	6 white peppercorns
½ bayleaf	½ bayleaf
½ blade mace	½ blade mace
Few sprigs fresh thyme	Few sprigs fresh thyme
15g butter	½oz butter
15g flour	½oz flour
Salt	Salt
125g Gruyère cheese, grated	4oz Gruyère cheese, grated

Drop the prepared cabbage into boiling salted water and simmer 15 minutes. Drain and shred finely.

To make the sauce put the milk, onion, peppercorns, bayleaf, mace and thyme into a pan and simmer 15 minutes. Strain. Melt the butter and stir in the flour. Cook, stirring, for 1 minute. Stir in the strained milk and salt. Bring to the boil and simmer, stirring, until thick and smooth.

Put half the cabbage into a greased baking dish, coat with half the sauce and sprinkle with half the cheese. Repeat the layers. Put into a hot oven, 220°C/425°F, Gas Mark 7 for 20 minutes or until browned. If liked, mix crisply fried breadcrumbs with the cheese to add 'crunch'.
Serves 4

Marrow with Dill

Metric	Imperial
25g butter	1oz butter
2 shallots, chopped	2 shallots, chopped
50g mushrooms, sliced	2oz mushrooms, sliced
450g marrow, peeled, seeded and cubed	1lb marrow, peeled, seeded and cubed
Salt and freshly ground black pepper	Salt and freshly ground black pepper
Chopped fresh dill	Chopped fresh dill

Marrow benefits from the addition of a little extra flavour. It needs no extra liquid in cooking or its flavour will be lost.

Melt the butter and cook the prepared shallots slowly for a few minutes. Add the mushrooms and cook for a further 3 minutes. Add the marrow to the pan with salt and pepper, stir, cover with lid and cook slowly for 15 minutes, stirring once or twice. If the mixture in the pan is too moist, uncover, increase the heat and evaporate some of the liquid. Pour into a heated dish and sprinkle with chopped dill. An alternative garnish is chopped tomato flesh.
Serves 4

Salsify in Cream Sauce

Metric	Imperial
½–¾kg salsify	1–1½lb salsify
Lemon juice	Lemon juice
Cream sauce:	*Cream sauce:*
25g butter	1oz butter
25g flour	1oz flour
450ml mixed milk and cream	¾ pint mixed milk and cream
Salt and pepper	Salt and pepper
225g cooked peas, fresh or frozen	½lb cooked peas, fresh or frozen
1 × 15ml spoon chopped fresh mint	1tbsp chopped fresh mint

Sometimes called 'Poor Man's Asparagus', salsify should be used when young and not too large.

Scrape the salsify and rub with lemon juice to prevent discoloration. Cut into 5cm (2in) lengths, drop into boiling salted water and simmer 20 minutes or until tender. Drain. Meanwhile, melt the butter and stir in the flour. Cook, stirring, for 1 minute. Stir in the milk and cream and seasoning. Bring to the boil and simmer, stirring, until thick and smooth. The proportion of milk to cream depends upon personal taste. Add the salsify and peas to the sauce. Transfer to a heated dish and sprinkle with mint.
Serves 4

Accompaniments

Damson Sauce

Metric
2kg damsons
½kg onions, chopped
600ml vinegar
25g salt
5g ground cinnamon
15g fresh root ginger, bruised
5g whole allspice
225g sugar

Imperial
4lb damsons
1lb onions, chopped
1 pint vinegar
1oz salt
¼oz ground cinnamon
½oz fresh root ginger, bruised
¼oz whole allspice
½lb sugar

Plums can be used instead of damsons in which case the amount of cinnamon must be reduced.
Wash the damsons and put into a pan with the prepared onions, vinegar, salt, cinnamon and the ginger and allspice tied in muslin. Simmer about 45 minutes, stirring from time to time, to break up the flesh of the damsons. Remove spices and rub the pulp through a sieve. Return to the rinsed pan, add the sugar and simmer a further 45 minutes or until sauce is a thick pouring consistency. Pour into heated jars and seal while hot. Allow to mature for 1 to 2 months before using.
Makes about 1½ pints

Horseradish Sauce with Walnuts

Metric
2 × 15ml spoons horseradish, freshly grated
150ml soured cream
12 walnut halves, finely chopped
Salt and pepper

Imperial
2tbsps horseradish, freshly grated
¼ pint soured cream
12 walnut halves, finely chopped
Salt and pepper

A new version of an old favourite to serve with the Sunday roast beef joint. It is also good with cold, pickled mackerel and herrings.
Fold the freshly prepared horseradish into the soured cream with the nuts and seasoning. Taste and add a little more horseradish if necessary.
Makes about 300ml (½ pint) sauce

Pesto or Pistou

Metric
50g fresh basil leaves
3 cloves garlic, peeled
Salt
125g Gruyère cheese
3 × 15ml spoons olive oil

Imperial
2oz fresh basil leaves
3 cloves garlic, peeled
Salt
4oz Gruyère cheese
3tbsps olive oil

A savoury sauce from the areas of the Italian and French Rivieras. Add 1 × 15ml spoon (1tbsp) or more to vegetable soups such as minestrone and to meat sauces served with pasta.
Put the basil, garlic and salt into a mortar and pound together very well. Cut the cheese into very thin strips (with a potato peeler) and add to the mortar alternately with the oil, pounding well between each addition. This should give a creamy sauce which is just a little difficult to pour. If liked, work in 25g (1oz) chopped walnuts.
Makes 4–6 × 15ml spoons (4–5 tbsps) sauce

Tarragon and Lemon Dressing

Metric
Grated rind of ½ lemon
150ml olive oil
3 × 15ml spoons lemon juice
1 × 5ml spoon sugar
1 × 5ml spoon chopped fresh tarragon
Salt and pepper

Imperial
Grated rind of ½ lemon
¼ pint olive oil
3tbsps lemon juice
1tsp sugar
1tsp chopped fresh tarragon
Salt and pepper

This can be used as a dressing for salads to serve with chicken, veal, rabbit, fish and shellfish. It can also be used as a marinade for those meats and fishes.
Mix the lemon rind and oil together with a wooden spoon. Beat in the lemon juice, sugar, tarragon, salt and pepper, in that order.
Makes 225ml (8floz) dressing

Sauces (clockwise): pesto, horseradish, damson, tarragon and lemon dressing

Walnut and Herb Cheese Spread

Metric
225g cream cheese
3 × 15ml spoons soured cream
40g walnuts, finely chopped
2 × 5ml spoons chopped
    fresh chives
2 × 5ml spoons chopped
    fresh tarragon or thyme
Salt
Pinch of cayenne pepper

Imperial
½lb cream cheese
3tbsps soured cream
1½oz walnuts, finely chopped
2tsps chopped fresh chives
2tsps chopped fresh tarragon
    or thyme
Salt
Pinch of cayenne pepper

A good spread to use in sandwiches and to spread on savoury scones. Spread thickly on bread it can form a very good base for open sandwiches with a variety of toppings.
Soften the cream cheese with a wooden spoon and then work in the other ingredients in the order given.
Makes 275g (10oz) spread

Hot Tomato Sauce

Metric
1½kg ripe tomatoes
450ml vinegar
125g onions, chopped
2 cloves garlic, crushed
2 dried or 4 fresh chillis
20g salt
75g granulated sugar
Pinch of cayenne pepper
1 medium red pepper,
    seeded and sliced
Very small piece fresh root
    ginger, bruised

Imperial
3lb ripe tomatoes
¾ pint vinegar
4oz onions, chopped
2 cloves garlic, crushed
2 dried or 4 fresh chillis
¾oz salt
3oz granulated sugar
Pinch of cayenne pepper
1 medium red pepper, seeded
    and sliced
Very small piece fresh root
    ginger, bruised

There are three quite definite stages in the making of this sauce: 1) Softening the tomatoes; 2) Cooking with the flavourings; 3) Cooking to thicken the sauce.
Put the tomatoes into a casserole, cover with the lid and cook at 140°C/275°F, mark 1 for 1½ hours or until very soft. Transfer to a pan, add all the other ingredients, cover with a lid and cook for 1 hour. Remove chillis and ginger and rub through a non-metal sieve. If possible, put through a blender first. Return to the rinsed pan and cook for a further hour or until thick. Pour into heated jars and seal while still hot. Leave for 1–2 months to mature.
Makes about 900ml (1½ pints)

Fresh Vegetable Sauce

Metric
½ red or green pepper,
    seeded and chopped
1 very small onion, chopped
1 stalk celery, chopped
3 tomatoes, skinned and
    chopped
1 sprig of thyme
2 × 15ml spoons chopped
    parsley
Salt and pepper
1 clove garlic, crushed,
    optional
Thin strip lemon rind

Imperial
½ red or green pepper,
    seeded and chopped
1 very small onion, chopped
1 stalk celery, chopped
3 tomatoes, skinned and
    chopped
1 sprig of thyme
2tbsps chopped parsley
Salt and pepper
1 clove garlic, crushed,
    optional
Thin strip lemon rind

This sauce should be used as soon as possible after preparation. It is good served with bacon and fried eggs, boiled potatoes, braised vegetables and most fried foods.
Put all the ingredients into a blender and blend for 1 minute. Turn out and chill. This sauce can also be made by chopping all the ingredients very, very finely.
Makes 150ml (¼ pint) sauce

Celery, Tomato and Apple Stuffing

Metric
25g butter
1 large onion, chopped
2 stalks celery, chopped
2 large cooking apples, peeled
    cored and sliced
175g fresh breadcrumbs
15g caster sugar
1 × 15ml spoon chopped fresh
    thyme
2 × 5ml spoons chopped
    parsley
Salt and pepper
2 large tomatoes, skinned and
    chopped

Imperial
1oz butter
1 large onion, chopped
2 stalks celery, chopped
2 large cooking apples, peeled,
    cored and sliced
6oz fresh breadcrumbs
½oz caster sugar
1tbsp chopped fresh thyme
2tsps chopped parsley
Salt and pepper
2 large tomatoes, skinned and
    chopped

Use to stuff a duck or boned joint of pork; double the quantities for goose.
Melt the butter and fry the onion and celery until lightly browned. Stir in the prepared apples and cook for 5 minutes. Mix the breadcrumbs, sugar and herbs together; season with salt and pepper. Add the onion mixture and chopped tomatoes and mix well.

(Clockwise): hot tomato sauce, walnut and herb cheese spread, celery, tomato and apple stuffing, fresh vegetable sauce

Grated Carrot Stuffing

Metric	Imperial	
50g fresh white breadcrumbs	2oz fresh white breadcrumbs	*A good stuffing for meat, especially for liver or chicken.*
50g pork fat, minced	2oz pork fat, minced	Mix all the ingredients together, adding enough apricot juice to
1 small carrot, peeled and grated	1 small carrot, peeled and grated	moisten the mixture so it will hold together.
½ small onion, grated	½ small onion, grated	*Makes 275g (10oz) stuffing*
50g stewed apricots, chopped	2oz stewed apricots, chopped	
1 × 2.5ml spoon ground ginger	½tsp ground ginger	
Salt and pepper	Salt and pepper	
Approx. 2 × 15ml spoons apricot juice	Approx. 2tbsps apricot juice	

Rouget Sauce*

Metric	Imperial	
225g red currants, washed	½lb red currants, washed	*A simple but effective sauce, this can be used in a variety of sweet dishes. It is especially good with icecream and can replace the traditional sauce in peach melba.*
225g raspberries, washed	½lb raspberries, washed	Simmer the redcurrants, raspberries and sugar together for 10–12
150g caster sugar	5oz caster sugar	minutes. Cool a little and then blend until smooth. Return to the
2 × 5ml spoons arrowroot	2tsps arrowroot	rinsed pan with the arrowroot mixed to a smooth paste with the
1 × 15ml spoon cold water	1tbsp water	water. Bring to the boil and boil, stirring, for 3 minutes. Allow to cool, stirring from time to time to prevent a skin forming.
		To freeze: Pour into small containers, seal and freeze.
		To thaw: In the refrigerator for 3–4 hours. Beat before using.
		Makes 600ml (1 pint) sauce

Rice, Nut and Carrot Stuffing

Metric	Imperial	
25g butter	1oz butter	*Use with poultry, pork or lamb.*
50g bacon, rinded and chopped	2oz bacon, rinded and chopped	Melt the butter and fry the bacon and onion for 5–7 minutes until lightly browned. Mix in the rice, chicken liver, nuts and carrots
1 large onion, chopped	1 large onion, chopped	together, add the marjoram and season. Use a little beaten egg to
50g rice, cooked	2oz rice, cooked	bind the ingredients together.
1 chicken liver, chopped	1 chicken liver, chopped	*Makes 275g (10oz) stuffing*
50g hazelnuts, chopped	2oz hazelnuts, chopped	
2 large carrots, grated	2 large carrots, grated	
1 × 15ml spoon chopped fresh marjoram	1 tbsp chopped fresh marjoram	
Salt and pepper	Salt and pepper	
Beaten egg to bind	Beaten egg to bind	

Fresh Apricot Stuffing

Metric	Imperial	
175g fresh apricots, stoned	6oz fresh apricots, stoned	*This stuffing is sufficient for a crown roast of lamb and gives a delicious extra flavour to the meat. It is, of course, good with any cut of lamb.*
100g lamb's liver, lightly fried	4oz lamb's liver, lightly fried	Chop the apricots and the liver together. Fold in the rice, grated
75g rice, boiled	3oz rice, boiled	onion, parsley and seasonings. For variation, fresh white bread-
1 small onion, grated	1 small onion, grated	crumbs can replace the rice. The amount will depend upon the
2 × 15ml spoons chopped parsley	2tbsps chopped parsley	ripeness of the fruit but start with 75g (3oz).
Salt and pepper	Salt and pepper	

(Clockwise): grated carrot stuffing, rice and carrot stuffing, rouget sauce

Herb Butters*

Metric	Imperial
125g butter	4oz butter
2–4 × 5ml spoons chopped fresh herbs, or 1–2 × 5ml spoons dried herbs	2–4tsps chopped fresh herbs, or 1–2tsps dried herbs
Lemon juice	Lemon juice

A thin round of flavoured butter adds a delightful touch to many grilled foods. Use to butter the bread for open sandwiches, put on baked jacket potatoes, serve with hot toast, melt small quantities for tossing cooked vegetables, etc.

Allow the butter to soften in a warm kitchen, then cream with a wooden spoon. Gradually beat in the herbs (if using dried ones soak them for ½ hour in a little lemon juice). Cream in a little lemon juice. Form into a roll 2.5–4cm in diameter (1–1½in diameter), wrap in a plastic film and leave 2–4 hours for the flavours to blend. *Or* make into a flat pack and cut into cubes for serving.

To freeze Cut roll into slices and re-form with small pieces of greaseproof paper to separate. Overwrap. Store up to 3 months.

To thaw Separate pieces and leave on a plate for about ½ hour.

Makes 125g (4oz) butter

Herbs to use Experiment with butters made with single herbs or by mixing two or three. Other flavours can be added, e.g. anchovy with parsley, tomato with basil. Garlic butter is good and so is butter containing chopped spring onions, and other herbs may be mixed with these two flavours.

Garlic Bread with Herbs

Metric	Imperial
75g butter	3oz butter
2–4 cloves garlic, crushed	2–4 cloves garlic, crushed
2–4 × 5ml spoons chopped fresh herbs, or 1–2 × 5ml spoons dried herbs	2–4tsps chopped fresh herbs, or 1–2tsps dried herbs
1 loaf French bread	1 loaf French bread

Use butter softened in a warm kitchen. Beat with a wooden spoon, gradually beating in the garlic and herbs. Slice the loaf downwards nearly through and spread each slice with a little butter. Wrap tightly in foil and, if possible, allow to stand for an hour or so before baking. Bake at 200°C/400°F, Gas Mark 6 for 10–15 minutes. Serve hot or cold with appropriate starters or soups.

Serves 4–6

Mayonnaise Verte

Metric	Imperial
50g sorrel	2oz sorrel
25g spinach	1oz spinach
25g parsley or chervil	1oz parsley or chervil
300ml mayonnaise	½ pint mayonnaise

Sorrel is treated in the same way as spinach but it has a slightly bitter flavour, which makes this mayonnaise an excellent one to serve with fish, especially shellfish.

After removing thick stems cook the sorrel, spinach and parsley or chervil into boiling water for about 2 minutes. Strain and squeeze out as much liquid as possible. Chop well and dry in absorbent kitchen paper. Stir into the mayonnaise.

Makes 300ml (½ pint) mayonnaise

Herb Bread

Metric	Imperial
450g wholemeal flour	1lb wholemeal flour
1 × 5ml spoon salt	1tsp salt
2 × 15ml spoons chopped fresh herbs	2tbsps chopped fresh herbs
1 medium onion, chopped and lightly fried, optional	1 medium onion, chopped and lightly fried, optional
Scant 450ml warm water	Scant ¾ pint warm water
2 × 5ml spoons dried yeast	2tsps dried yeast
1 × 5ml spoon sugar	1tsp sugar

Herb breads are delicious served with savoury foods such as a hot, thick vegetable soup for a light mid-day or supper dish. Serve, instead of potatoes, with meat or poultry roasts, casseroles and stews. They are very good with strongly flavoured cheeses.

Sift the flour and salt into a bowl. Mix in the herbs and the onion, if used. Put into a warm place.

Put ¼ pint of the water into a small basin and stir in the yeast and sugar. Leave in a warm place until frothy (about 20 minutes). Pour into the centre of the flour with the remaining water and mix well. Turn out on to a floured board and knead for about 3 minutes. Put into a well-greased loaf tin, put into a plastic bag, seal to exclude draughts and leave in a warm place to rise. When the dough fills the tin, bake at 200°C, 425°F, Gas Mark 7 for 45 minutes.

Makes 1 loaf

Desserts

Loganberry Cheesecake

Metric	Imperial
125g digestive biscuit crumbs	4oz digestive biscuit crumbs
25g demerara sugar	1oz demerara sugar
25g nuts, chopped	1oz nuts, chopped
50g butter, melted	2oz butter, melted
2 eggs, separated	2 eggs, separated
75g sugar	3oz sugar
Pinch of salt	Pinch of salt
225g loganberries	½lb loganberries
15g powdered unflavoured gelatine	½oz powdered unflavoured gelatine
3 × 15ml spoons water	3tbsps water
350g cottage cheese, sieved	¾lb cottage cheese, sieved
150ml double cream, whipped until stiff	¼ pint double cream, whipped until stiff
Extra loganberries	Extra loganberries

Mix the crumbs, demerara sugar, nuts and butter together. Press firmly into the base of a 20cm (8in) spring form or loose-bottomed tin, covered with a circle of foil. Whisk the egg yolks, sugar and salt in a basin over a pan of hot, but not boiling, water until thick and creamy and the whisk leaves a definite trail. Cool, whisking occasionally. Rub the loganberries through a sieve. Dissolve the gelatine in the water. Whisk the egg whites until stiff. Mix the yolks, fruit, gelatine and cottage cheese together and fold in the whites and half the cream. Pour into the prepared tin and smooth over the top. When set, decorate with the reserved cream and decorate with the extra fruit.
Serves 8–10

Plum Slices*

Metric	Imperial
Shortcrust pastry made from 175g flour and 75g fat	Shortcrust pastry made from 6oz flour and 3oz fat
½kg ripe plums, halved and stoned	1lb ripe plums, halved and stoned
2 eggs, separated	2 eggs, separated
65g caster sugar	2½oz caster sugar
50g self-raising flour	2oz self-raising flour
Pinch of salt	Pinch of salt
Vanilla essence	Vanilla essence
Icing sugar	Icing sugar

Use the pastry to line a tin approx. 18cm × 23cm (7in × 9in). Prick the base. Bake blind for 15 minutes at 200°C/400°F, Gas Mark 6, until very lightly browned. Arrange the plum halves on the pastry with the cut sides uppermost. If they are not sweet enough, dip them in sugar first. Whisk the egg whites until very stiff, whisk in the yolks, one at a time, and then the sugar, keeping the mixture as stiff as possible. Fold in the flour, sifted with the salt, and a few drops of vanilla essence. Spread evenly over the plums, and bake for 35–40 minutes, or until the sponge is well risen and golden brown. Turn out on to a wire tray and allow to cool. Sprinkle with icing sugar before serving with cream or custard.
To freeze Wrap in foil or place in a polythene bag, seal, label and freeze.
To serve Place the frozen sponge in a hot oven, 220°C/425°F, Gas Mark 7, for 20 minutes, then reduce temperature to moderate, 180°C/350°F, Gas Mark 4, for a further 15–20 minutes. Serve as above.
Serves 6

Blackberry and Apple Sponge

Metric	Imperial
125g butter	4oz butter
125g caster sugar	4oz caster sugar
2 eggs, beaten	2 eggs, beaten
Few drops vanilla essence	Few drops vanilla essence
175g self-raising flour, sifted	6oz self-raising flour, sifted
450g cooking apples, peeled, cored, sliced and cooked	1lb cooking apples, peeled, cored, sliced and cooked
225g blackberries, cooked	½lb blackberries, cooked
Juice of ½ lemon	Juice of ½ lemon
125g sugar	4oz sugar

Cream the butter and caster sugar together until light and fluffy. Gradually add the beaten eggs and essence, beating well between each addition. Using a metal spoon, fold in the flour. Mix the fruit, lemon juice and sugar together. Put 4 × 15ml spoons (4tbsps) in the bottom of a greased 700g (1½lb) pudding basin. Spoon in the sponge mixture, cover with greased greaseproof paper or foil and secure with string. Steam for 1½ hours. Reheat rest of apple and blackberry mixture and serve with pudding.
Serves 4

Stuffed Apple Jelly

Metric	Imperial
6 small sweet dessert apples	6 small sweet dessert apples
600ml water	1 pint water
50g sugar	2oz sugar
15g angelica, chopped	½oz angelica, chopped
25g glacé cherries, chopped	1oz glacé cherries, chopped
25g nuts, chopped	1oz nuts, chopped
Honey	Honey
Packet of orange or greengage jelly	Packet of orange or greengage jelly
150ml double cream	¼ pint double cream

Peel and core the apples and put at once into the water and sugar at simmering point. Cover the pan and simmer carefully for about 10 minutes, then remove from heat and leave until the apples are soft but still whole. This will take a further 10–15 minutes. Lift out and arrange in serving dish. Mix the angelica, cherries and nuts with a little honey, and use to stuff the apples. Make up the jelly as directed on the packet, using the syrup in which the apples were cooked. When almost set, spoon it over the apples until each is completely coated; pour the rest into the dish. Whisk the cream until stiff and sweeten to taste with a little sugar. Use the cream to decorate the top of the apples.

For a more substantial sweet, put a layer of sponge or plain cake in the bottom of the dish.

Serves 6

Coffee and Walnut Icecream*

Metric	Imperial
150ml milk	¼ pint milk
40g sugar	1½oz sugar
2 egg yolks	2 egg yolks
2 × 5ml spoons powdered coffee, dissolved in 2 × 5ml spoons hot water	2tsps powdered coffee, dissolved in 2tsps hot water
150ml double cream, lightly whipped	¼ pint double cream, lightly whipped
75g walnuts, chopped	3oz walnuts, chopped

Set the freezer or refrigerator at its lowest setting. Heat the milk and sugar together and pour on to the egg yolks, stirring well. Return the mixture to the pan and cook over very gentle heat, stirring all the time until the custard thickens. Strain and add the dissolved coffee. Allow the mixture to cool, then fold in the lightly whipped cream and chopped walnuts. Pour into an ice-cube tray, and freeze. When the icecream is half set, remove from the freezer, turn into a cool bowl, and whisk well. Return to the tray and allow to freeze until set.

Serves 4

Strawberry Sorbet*

Metric	Imperial
225g loaf or granulated sugar	½lb loaf or granulated sugar
600ml water	1 pint water
700g strawberries	1½lb strawberries
2 egg whites	2 egg whites
Food colouring if necessary	Food colouring if necessary

Set the freezer or refrigerator at its lowest setting. Dissolve the sugar in the water, gradually bring to the boil, and boil steadily for 10 minutes, or until the temperature is 104°C/220°F. Allow to cool. Pass the fruit through a sieve, or purée in a blender, make up to 600ml (1 pint) with water, if necessary. Add to the syrup. Pour into an ice tray and half freeze. Remove from freezer and beat well. Fold in the stiffly beaten egg whites. If necessary, stir in a little red food colouring. Return to the tray and continue freezing.

Serves 4–6

Special Fruit Trifle

Metric	Imperial
125g sponge cake	4oz sponge cake
2–3 × 15ml spoons dry white wine	2–3tbsps dry white wine
225g strawberries, fresh or frozen and thawed	½lb strawberries, fresh or frozen, thawed
225g raspberries, fresh or frozen and thawed	½lb raspberries, fresh or frozen, thawed
125g caster sugar	4oz caster sugar
300ml made custard	½ pint made custard
300ml double cream, whipped	½ pint double cream, whipped
75–125g mixed raspberries and strawberries to decorate	3–4oz mixed raspberries and strawberries to decorate

Cut up the sponge cake and use to line the base of a 20cm (8in) glass bowl. Spoon over the wine, ensuring that all the sponge is covered. Allow to stand for 20 minutes. Mix the strawberries, raspberries and sugar together; leave until the sugar is absorbed by the fruit, about 30 minutes. Arrange the fruit on top of the sponge cake. Spoon over the custard. Pipe the whipped cream in rosettes on top, and decorate with the whole strawberries and raspberries.

Serves 4–6

Somerset Flan

Metric
Shortcrust pastry made from
    175g flour and 75g fat
450ml water
140g sugar
½kg cooking apples
2 eggs
25g flour
25g almonds, chopped
Icing sugar

Imperial
Shortcrust pastry made from
    6oz flour and 3oz fat
¾ pint water
5½oz sugar
1lb cooking apples
2 eggs
1oz flour
1oz almonds, chopped
Icing sugar

Use the pastry to line an 18cm (7in) fluted flan ring. Line with greaseproof paper or foil, fill with beans and bake blind for 25 minutes at 200°C/400°F, Gas Mark 6, removing beans and paper after about 15 minutes. Bring the water to the boil and add 75g (3oz) of the sugar. Peel and core the apples, cut into 4, 6 or 8 sections according to size, and drop immediately into the syrup. Cook until soft but not broken, drain and leave until cold. Measure syrup, and if necessary make up to 300ml (½ pint) with hot water. Beat the eggs and remaining sugar together, then beat in flour. Add hot syrup a little at a time, return to the pan, and heat and stir until thick. Arrange apples in flan case and pour egg mixture over. Smooth the top, sprinkle with almonds and cover with icing sugar. Brown under a hot grill, and serve hot or cold, with cream if liked.
Serves 6

Pears in Red Wine*

Metric
225g sugar
5cm cinnamon stick
2 cloves
2 strips orange peel
2 strips lemon peel
½ bottle red wine
6 firm pears
2 × 5ml spoons arrowroot

Imperial
½lb sugar
2in cinnamon stick
2 cloves
2 strips orange peel
2 strips lemon peel
½ bottle red wine
6 firm pears
2tsps arrowroot

Put the sugar, cinnamon, cloves, peel and wine in a pan, and heat slowly; increase heat and boil for 1 minute. Peel the pears, leaving stalks on but removing the 'eye' from the bottom. Place at once in the prepared syrup. Cover pan and poach pears for about 30 minutes until tender. Remove pears from the pan, strain the syrup, check the quantity and if necessary reduce the amount to 300ml (½ pint). Mix the arrowroot with a little water, add to the syrup, and stir until boiling; then cook until quite clear. Arrange the pears in a serving dish and spoon over wine syrup. Serve cold with whipped cream.
To freeze Freeze the pears and sauce together in waxed or plastic containers and cover with a lid or foil.
To serve Thaw at room temperature for 5–6 hours.
Serves 6

Peach and Apple Soufflé*

Metric
700g cooking apples, peeled,
    cored and sliced
9 × 15ml spoons water
4 fresh ripe peaches, skinned
    and stoned
6 eggs, separated
275g caster sugar
2 × 15ml spoons lemon juice
5 × 5ml spoons powdered
    gelatine
2 × 15ml spoons orange
    liqueur
150ml single cream
Few frosted grapes

Imperial
1½lb cooking apples, peeled,
    cored and sliced
9tbsps water
4 fresh ripe peaches, skinned
    and stoned
6 eggs, separated
10oz caster sugar
2tbsps lemon juice
5tsps powdered gelatine
2tbsps orange liqueur
¼ pint single cream
Few frosted grapes

Prepare a 1.4 litre (2½ pint) soufflé dish, by tying a double band of greaseproof paper round the outside of dish, to stand 7.5cm (3in) above the rim. Stew the apples in 6 × 15ml spoons (6tbsps) of the water until soft. Cool. Put the apples and peaches through a sieve or purée in a blender. Place a bowl over a pan of hot water with the egg yolks, sugar and lemon juice; whisk until very thick and creamy. Remove from the heat and whisk until cool. Dissolve the gelatine in the remaining water, in a basin over hot water. Whisk the fruit purée, gelatine and orange liqueur into the egg mixture. Whip the cream and fold into the mixture. Finally, stiffly beat the egg whites and fold in. Turn into the prepared dish and chill until set. Using a knife, remove the paper collar from the soufflé. Decorate with frosted grapes (see page 88).
To freeze Open freeze, undecorated; when frozen put in two polythene bags, one inside the other. Seal and label. Take care that the soufflé does not get squashed.
To serve: Allow 14 hours in the refrigerator or 6–8 hours at room temperature.
Serves 6–8

Greengage Crumble*

Metric	Imperial
700g greengages, stoned	1½lb greengages, stoned
175–200g caster sugar	6–7oz caster sugar
75g butter	3oz butter
175g flour	6oz flour

Arrange the fruit in an ovenproof dish; sprinkle with 75–100g (6–7oz) of the sugar. Rub the fat into the flour until mixture resembles fine breadcrumbs. Stir in the remaining sugar. Sprinkle crumble over the fruit; use a fork to make a pretty decoration. Bake at 200°C/400°F, Gas Mark 6 for 40 minutes or until golden brown.
To freeze Leave unbaked. Cover with foil and freeze.
To serve Bake from frozen at 180°C/350°F, Gas Mark 4 for 1¼–1½ hours, until golden brown and cooked through.
Serves 4

Charlotte Russe

Metric	Imperial
150ml lemon jelly, cool but not set	¼ pint lemon jelly, cool but not set
1 tangerine, skinned and segmented	1 tangerine, skinned and segmented
Candied angelica, cut into leaves	Candied angelica, cut into leaves
22 boudoir sponge biscuits	22 boudoir sponge biscuits
1 egg white, beaten	1 egg white, beaten
15g powdered unflavoured gelatine	½oz powdered unflavoured gelatine
2 × 15ml spoons water	2tbsps water
600ml double cream, lightly whipped	1 pint double cream, lightly whipped
300ml made custard, cooled	½ pint made custard, cooled
2 × 15ml spoons dry white wine	2 tablespoons dry white wine
Rind and juice of 3 lemons	Rind and juice of 3 lemons
50–75g caster sugar	2–3oz caster sugar

Line the base of a 1.1 litre (2 pint) tin with half the jelly, and allow to set. Arrange the tangerine segments and angelica leaves in an attractive pattern on the jelly. Spoon over the remaining jelly, and allow to set. Trim the sponge biscuits, brush them with beaten egg white, and arrange round the sides of the tin. Put the gelatine and water in a basin over a pan of hot water, and dissolve. Mix the whipped cream, custard, wine, juice and rind of lemons together, and stir in the gelatine. Stir in the sugar, and pour the mixture into the prepared tin. Chill until set. Turn out on to a plate and decorate with a red ribbon.
Serves 4–6

Orange and Apricot Mousse*

Metric	Imperial
700g fresh apricots, stoned	1½lb fresh apricots, stoned
150g sugar	5oz sugar
4 × 15ml spoons water	4tbsps water
Grated rind and juice of 2 oranges	Grated rind and juice of 2 oranges
15g powdered unflavoured gelatine	½oz powdered unflavoured gelatine
150ml double cream, whipped	¼ pint double cream, whipped
3 egg whites, stiffly beaten	3 egg whites, stiffly beaten
To decorate:	*To decorate:*
150ml double cream, whipped	¼ pint double cream, whipped
1 nectarine, stoned and sliced	1 nectarine, stoned and sliced

Put the apricots in a pan, add the sugar and half the water, bring to the boil, cover and simmer for 12–15 minutes until the apricots are soft. Cool, put in a blender or rub through a sieve. Mix the purée with the orange rind and juice. Dissolve gelatine in the remaining water in a basin over a pan of hot water and stir into the fruit mixture. Fold in the cream and egg whites. Pour into a serving dish. Chill until set. Decorate with whipped cream, and slices of nectarine.
To freeze Open freeze, then wrap in foil, seal, label and return to the freezer.
To serve Thaw at room temperature for 5–6 hours. Decorate as above after thawing.
Serves 4–6

Yorkshire Apple Tart

Metric	Imperial
Shortcrust pastry made from 275g flour and 150g fat	Shortcrust pastry made from 10oz flour and 5oz fat
350g cooking apples, peeled, cored and sliced	¾lb cooking apples, peeled, cored and sliced
2 × 15ml spoons sugar	2tbsps sugar
1 × 15ml spoon water	1tbsp water
Little milk and sugar to glaze	Little milk and sugar to glaze
125g strong cheese, sliced	4oz strong cheese, sliced

Line a 20cm (8in) flan ring with two-thirds of the pastry. Fill the centre with the apples, add the sugar, and spoon over the water. Cover with the remaining pastry, and seal the edges. Brush the top with a little milk and sprinkle with sugar. Bake at 190°C/375°F, Gas Mark 5, for 20–25 minutes until the crust is firm and lightly browned. Allow to cool. Carefully remove the top crust using a sharp knife. Arrange the cheese on top of the apples. Replace the crust. Return to the oven and bake for a further 10–15 minutes until the cheese has just melted. Serve warm with whipped cream.
Serves 4–6

Rhubarb Fool

700g rhubarb, trimmed and
  cut into pieces
125–150g sugar, depending
  on taste
150ml made custard
150ml double cream, whipped
To decorate:
150ml double cream, whipped
Chopped nuts

Imperial
1½lb rhubarb, trimmed and
  cut into pieces
4–5oz sugar, depending on
  taste
¼ pint made custard
¼ pint double cream, whipped
To decorate:
¼ pint double cream, whipped
Chopped nuts

Stew the rhubarb in a little water until quite tender, about 10–12 minutes. Add the sugar to taste and cool. Rub the fruit through a sieve or purée in a blender. Stir the custard into the fruit purée. Fold in the whipped cream. Pour into individual dishes or a serving dish. Decorate with whipped cream and nuts and serve with home-made shortbread, sponge fingers, or a favourite sweet biscuit.
Serves 4

Summer Pudding*

Metric
2 × 15ml spoons water
150g sugar
450g red, black and white
  currants, washed and
  stringed
175g plain sponge cake,
  cut in thin slices
Whipped cream

Imperial
2tbsps water
5oz sugar
1lb red, black and white
  currants, washed and
  stringed
6oz plain sponge cake, cut in
  thin slices
Whipped cream

Stir the water and sugar together in a pan, and slowly bring to the boil; boil for 2 minutes. Add prepared fruit and stew gently until it is soft but still retains its shape. Cool. Use two-thirds of the sponge cake to line a 900ml (1½ pint) pudding basin and pour in the fruit and juices. Fill with the remaining sponge cake, cover with a saucer with a weight on top of the pudding and leave overnight in a cool place. Serve with whipped cream.
To freeze Remove saucer, cover with foil and freeze.
To serve Thaw at room temperature for 5–6 hours, turn out and serve with whipped cream.
Serves 4–6

Grape Crème Brûlée

Metric
600ml double cream
1 vanilla pod
6 egg yolks
4 × 15ml spoons caster sugar
225g black or white grapes,
  halved and pipped
25g icing sugar, sifted

Imperial
1 pint double cream
1 vanilla pod
6 egg yolks
4tbsps caster sugar
½lb black or white grapes,
  halved and pipped
1oz icing sugar, sifted

Put the cream and vanilla pod in a double saucepan. Cover and heat gently until just below boiling point. Remove vanilla pod. Mix the egg yolks and sugar together. Pour the cream on to the egg mixture and stir well. Return to the pan and stir until thickened; do not allow to boil. Arrange the grapes in a flameproof dish and strain over the cream and egg mixture. Put the dish into a roasting tin containing water and bake in a slow oven 150°C/300°F, Gas Mark 2 for 1–1½ hours until firm but not coloured. Cool and refrigerate for several hours, or overnight. Heat the grill and dust the top of the brûlée with the icing sugar. Put under the grill for a few seconds until the top is golden brown. Cool thoroughly and serve chilled.
Serves 4–6

Cherries Jubilee

Metric
450g dark red cherries, pitted
300ml water
4–5 × 15ml spoons sugar
2.5cm cinnamon stick
Juice and grated rind of
  ½ orange
2 × 5ml spoons cornflour
4 × 15ml spoons cognac
4 × 15ml spoons cherry
  brandy
Vanilla icecream

Imperial
1lb dark red cherries, pitted
½ pint water
4–5tbsps sugar
1in cinnamon stick
Juice and grated rind of
  ½ orange
2tsps cornflour
4tbsps cognac
4tbsps cherry brandy
Vanilla icecream

Put the cherries in a pan, add the water, bring to the boil and simmer for 2 minutes, until the cherries are tender but still whole. Add the sugar and allow to dissolve. Strain the juice and return to the pan. Add the cinnamon and orange rind. Blend the cornflour with the orange juice; add to the pan. Bring to the boil, stirring, and boil rapidly for 5 minutes, stirring occasionally until the sauce is reduced to a coating consistency. Add the cherries and heat through. Discard cinnamon stick. Heat cognac and cherry brandy and pour over cherries. Ignite, and when the flames have died down pour hot mixture over individual portions of icecream.
Serves 4

Rhubarb fool with cherries jubilee

Orange and Gooseberry Pancakes

Metric	Imperial
125g flour	4oz flour
Pinch of salt	Pinch of salt
1 egg	1 egg
300ml mixed milk and water	½ pint mixed milk and water
450g fresh or frozen and thawed gooseberries	1lb fresh or frozen and thawed gooseberries
Juice and grated rind of 1 orange	Juice and grated rind of 1 orange
75–125g sugar	3–4oz sugar
Lard or oil for frying	Lard or oil for frying

Sift the flour and salt into a bowl and make a well in the centre; break in the egg. Add half the liquid and beat the mixture until smooth. Add the remaining liquid gradually and beat well until mixed and smooth.

To make the filling put the gooseberries, orange juice and rind in a pan, heat gently and simmer 5–7 minutes until the gooseberries are tender but still hold their shape. Stir in sufficient sugar to taste.

Heat a little fat in a frying pan, making sure that all surfaces of the pan are coated; pour off any excess fat. Pour or spoon just enough batter to cover the base of the pan thinly, and cook quickly until golden brown underneath. Turn with a palette knife or toss the pancake and cook the other side until golden. Turn out on to greaseproof paper on a plate, cover and keep hot in the oven. When all the batter is used fill the pancakes with the hot filling, fold into 3 and serve at once, sprinkled generously with sugar. Serve any surplus filling in a jug.

Serves 4

Apricot Shortcake

Metric	Imperial
75g butter	3oz butter
225g self-raising flour	½lb self-raising flour
1 × 1.25ml spoon salt	¼tsp salt
75g sugar	3oz sugar
1 egg, beaten	1 egg, beaten
1–2 × 15ml spoons milk	1–2tbsps milk
350–450g fresh apricots, halved and stoned	¾–1lb fresh apricots, halved and stoned
3–4 × 15ml spoons sugar for filling	3–4tbsps sugar for filling
300ml double cream, whipped	½ pint double cream, whipped

Grease a 20cm (8in) loose-bottomed cake tin. Rub the butter into the flour and salt until the mixture resembles fine breadcrumbs. Stir in the sugar. Add the egg a little at a time until the mixture binds together. If necessary, add a little milk. Carefully knead the mixture on a floured board until smooth. Form into a round and roll out until it measures 20cm (8in) across. Press it into the prepared tin, and refrigerate for 20 minutes. Meanwhile, stew the apricots in their own juice with the sugar for 10–12 minutes until they are just tender, but still hold their shape. Cool. Bake the shortcake at 190°C/375°F, Gas Mark 5, for 20 minutes until golden brown and firm. Cool for 10 minutes, then remove from the tin and cool on a wire tray. When completely cold, carefully split the cake into two layers, using a sharp knife. Spread half the shortcake with half the cream, arrange two-thirds of the apricots on top. Put the second shortcake round on top, and pile on the remaining cream. Decorate with the remainder of the apricots.

Serves 6–8

Strawberries Romanoff

Metric	Imperial
900g fresh strawberries	2lb fresh strawberries
6 × 15ml spoons icing sugar	6tbsps icing sugar
3 × 15ml spoons rum	3tbsps rum
3 × 15ml spoons orange liqueur	3tbsps orange liqueur
300ml double cream	½ pint double cream
3 × 15ml spoons brandy	3tbsps brandy

Hull the strawberries and place in a bowl. Sprinkle with 4 × 15ml spoons (4tbsps) icing sugar, the rum and orange liqueur and mix well. Cover and chill for at least 1 hour. One hour before serving, whip the cream with the remaining sugar and brandy until stiff. Stir into the strawberries, making sure that all the strawberries are coated with cream. Serve chilled.

Serves 6–8

Melon and Grape Jelly

Metric	Imperial
1 melon, halved and seeded	1 melon, halved and seeded
2 sharp eating apples, peeled, cored and sliced	2 sharp eating apples, peeled, cored and sliced
175g black grapes, halved and pipped	6oz black grapes, halved and pipped
Grated rind and juice of 2 limes	Grated rind and juice of 2 limes
15g powdered gelatine	½oz powdered gelatine
2 × 15ml spoons water	2tbsps water
4 × 15ml spoons honey	4tbsps honey

Scoop the melon into balls and mix with the apples and grapes; scoop out the remaining melon flesh and chop roughly. Add the grated rind and juice of limes to the melon balls and apples. Dissolve the gelatine in the water in a basin over a pan of hot water. Stir the gelatine into the fruit mixture and add the honey. Put the chopped melon in the bottom of the melon shells, spoon over the fruit and jelly mixture and put in a cool place to set. Serve cold, cut in slices, with whipped cream if liked.

Serves 4–6

Melon and grape jelly with apricot shortcake

Plum Roly Poly

Metric
350g fresh plums, halved and stoned
50g caster sugar
8 × 15ml spoons water
175g self-raising flour
1 × 1.25ml spoon salt
75g shredded suet
Little milk

Imperial
¾lb fresh plums, halved and stoned
2oz caster sugar
8tbsps water
6oz self-raising flour
¼tsp salt
3oz shredded suet
Little milk

Put the plums in a pan, add the sugar and 2 × 15ml spoons (2tbsps) of the water and heat gently, making sure that the sugar does not burn. Simmer for 5–10 minutes until the plums are tender. Cool. Sift the flour and salt into a bowl, add suet and mix well. Stir in enough of the remaining water to give a light and elastic dough; knead very lightly until smooth. Roll out to 20 × 25cm (8 × 10in). Spread the plums over the pastry leaving a finger's width clear along each edge. Brush the edges with milk and roll the pastry up starting from one short side. Place the roll on greased greaseproof paper and foil and wrap round loosely to allow room for expansion, making sure that the edges are well sealed. Steam the roly poly in a steamer over a pan of rapidly boiling water for 1½–2 hours. When cooked, remove paper and serve hot with custard.
Serves 4–6

Fruit Savarin

Metric
25g fresh yeast
6 × 15ml spoons warm milk
225g strong flour
1 × 2.5ml spoon salt
25g caster sugar
4 eggs, beaten
125g butter, softened
Rum syrup:
4 × 15ml spoons clear honey
4 × 15ml spoons water
2–3 × 15ml spoons rum
For the filling:
2 oranges, peeled and segmented
2 eating apples, cored and sliced
1 pear, peeled, cored and sliced
50g green grapes, halved and pipped
50g black grapes, halved and pipped
Juice of ½ lemon
50g sugar ⎰ made into a
150ml water ⎱ syrup by boiling for 5 minutes, then cooled

Imperial
1oz fresh yeast
6tbsps warm milk
½lb strong flour
½tsp salt
1oz caster sugar
4 eggs, beaten
4oz butter, softened
Rum syrup:
4tbsps clear honey
4tbsps water
2–3tbsps rum
For the filling:
2 oranges, peeled and segmented
2 eating apples, cored and sliced
1 pear, peeled, cored and sliced
2oz green grapes, halved and pipped
2oz black grapes, halved and pipped
Juice of ½ lemon
2oz sugar ⎰ made into a
¼ pint water ⎱ syrup by boiling for 5 minutes, then cooled

Lightly grease a savarin tin. Put the yeast, milk and 50g (2oz) of the flour in a bowl and blend until smooth. Allow to stand in a warm place until frothy, about 20 minutes. Add the remaining flour, the salt, sugar, eggs and butter and beat well for 4–5 minutes. Pour into tin and allow to rise in a warm place until it has doubled in size. Bake just above the centre of the oven at 200°C/400°F, Gas Mark 6, for about 40 minutes, or until golden brown and shrinking away from the sides of the tin. Turn out straight away on to a cooling tray and allow to cool. Mix the ingredients for the rum syrup; warm in a pan. Spoon over the savarin. Place on a serving dish. Mix all the fruits together for the filling, stir in the lemon juice and sugar syrup. Just before serving pile the fruit in the centre of the savarin. Serve any remaining fruit separately. Serve with whipped cream.
Serves 4–6

Hazelnut and Chestnut Meringue

Metric
450g chestnuts
175g sugar
2 × 15ml spoons rum
150ml double cream, lightly whipped
5 egg whites
275g caster sugar
125g hazelnuts, finely chopped
50g hazelnuts, chopped
Chocolate leaves to decorate

Imperial
1lb chestnuts
6oz sugar
2tbsps rum
¼ pint double cream, lightly whipped
5 egg whites
10oz caster sugar
4oz hazelnuts, finely chopped
2oz hazelnuts, chopped
Chocolate leaves to decorate

Prepare the chestnuts as for marrons glácés, see page 86 but cook them until tender. Mash with a potato masher, and while still hot stir in the rum and sugar. When cool fold in the cream. Draw a 20cm (8in) circle on a sheet of silicone paper, and place the paper on a baking sheet. Whisk the egg whites until very stiff, then whisk in half the caster sugar, keeping the mixture stiff. Fold in the remaining sugar and the finely chopped hazelnuts. Spread some of the meringue over the circle to form the base of the flan. Using a large star nozzle, pipe the remaining meringue round the edge of the flan to form an edge made of rosettes. Bake towards the bottom of the oven at 130°C/250°F, Gas Mark ¼–½, for 1½–2 hours until firm and just beginning to colour. Allow to cool, remove the paper and place the meringue on a serving dish. Add the chopped hazelnuts to the chestnut mixture, and pile into the centre of the basket. Decorate with chocolate leaves.
Serves 6–8

Hazelnut and chestnut meringue with fruit savarin

Drinks & Candied Fruits

Candying is the process of extracting moisture from fruits and replacing it with the sugar from a syrup in which they are soaked and which is made progressively stronger. The peel from citrus fruits, the stalks of angelica and chestnuts can be preserved in a similar way. During the soaking periods of 24 hours or longer, the moisture from the fruit dilutes the syrup a little. The syrup is then made stronger by adding extra sugar or by evaporating some of the liquid (boiling to get a higher temperature reading) before soaking again. Syrup left after candying can be stored in the refrigerator, diluted with fruit juice or water and used for fruit salad and for stewed fruit or for sweetening drinks.

Candied Fruits

These fruits should be candied when they are fully ripe so that their flavour is at its peak, but while still firm. Small fruit should be chosen in preference to large ones. Prick whole fruits such as plums, greengages, apricots and crabapples with a silver fork (to avoid discoloration), stone cherries and peel and halve peaches and pears, discarding stone or core. *Deal with each type of fruit separately.*

Simmer carefully in water until *just* tender (3–15 minutes), lift out and place in a bowl. Dissolve 175g (6oz) sugar, or half sugar and half glucose, in 300ml (½ pint) of the water in which the fruit was cooked, and pour over the fruit. Leave 24 hours. Drain off the syrup, add 50g (2oz) sugar, dissolve, bring to the boil and pour over the fruit. Repeat this on 5 more successive days.

Then add 75g (3oz) sugar to the syrup, dissolve, add the fruit and simmer 3 minutes. Pour back into bowl and leave 2 days. Repeat with a further 75g (3oz) sugar and leave 4 days. Drain, put on a wire tray and dry in a very cool oven 38–49°C/100–120°F until the surface is no longer sticky. (If your oven cannot be controlled at such a low temperature, heat it to 49°C/120°F, put in the fruit, shut the door, turn off the heat and leave in the cooling oven. This may have to be repeated over several days. A sugar thermometer can be used to check the oven heat.)

A sugar or crystallized finish can be obtained by dipping each piece of fruit into boiling water, draining quickly and then rolling in granulated sugar. If liked, food colouring can be added to the syrup to improve the appearance, especially that of cherries.

Candied fruit should not be stored under airtight conditions or it will go mouldy. Use small boxes of cardboard or wood with waxed paper to line the box and to separate the layers.

Candied Peel

Use well-washed and scrubbed skins of oranges, grapefruit, lemons and limes. Cut fruit into halves, squeeze out juice and remove pulp, or remove peel in quarters. If liked, cut peel into strips about 1cm (½in) wide. *Process each type of fruit separately.* The skins can be frozen until you have enough to make a boiling worthwhile.

Put into a pan, cover with cold water, bring to the boil, simmer 10 minutes and drain. For grapefruit, repeat this process twice more, then simmer until the peel is tender. The other peels also require a total simmering time of about 1 hour. Drain.

Using 450g (1lb) sugar, or half sugar and half glucose, to 600ml (1 pint) water, make a syrup and boil to 104°C/220°F on the sugar thermometer, add peel and leave over the lowest possible heat for a further hour. It is really keeping the syrup hot rather than allowing the temperature to rise more than a very little. Leave covered for 24 hours. Then boil to 107°C/226°F, leave 24 hours, boil to 109°C/228°F and leave 24–48 hours. Reheat, transfer peel to wire trays and dry as candied fruits.

Roll in sugar and store in airtight containers. Some of the thick final syrup can be poured into the hollows of halved or quartered peels and the colour of the peel can be accentuated by adding food colouring to the syrup.

The strips of peel can be served as sweetmeats. They taste even better if the white pith is scraped away after the peel has been simmered until tender.

Candied Angelica

Used to decorate sweet dishes, it is often cut into leaf shapes, or chopped. It can be added to cakes and biscuits.

Pick the stalks early in spring (early May) while young and tender and when the colour is bright. Remove the outer skin by putting into a bowl with 1 × 5ml spoon (1tsp) salt and pouring 600 ml (1 pint) boiling water over. After 15 minutes remove stalks, rinse, add to boiling water and cook gently for 5 minutes or until the skin can be scraped off. Cut into 5–7.5cm (2–3in) lengths.

Dissolve 450g (1lb) sugar, or half sugar and half glucose, in 600ml (1 pint) water, bring to the boil, simmer 5 minutes, pour over the angelica and leave overnight. On each of the next 6 or 7 days, drain off the syrup, bring to the boil, simmer 5 minutes, pour over the angelica and leave 24 hours. By this time the syrup should be as thick as honey. Leave to soak for a further 5 days. Then drain stalks and dry as Candied Fruits. Store in a dry place in airtight bottles. If the colour is pale add a few drops of green food colouring.

Marrons Glacés

Metric	Imperial
1½kg chestnuts	3lb chestnuts
1½kg sugar	3lb sugar
600ml water	1 pint water
Vanilla essence	Vanilla essence
Extra sugar	Extra sugar

Expensive to buy, these sweetmeats are so delicious they are worth spending the time it takes to make them.

Peel the chestnuts by cutting a cross into the top of each one with a sharp knife. Drop a few at a time into boiling water for 5 minutes, or bake in a moderate oven (180°C/350°F or Gas Mark 4). Remove both outer shells and inner skins.

Put peeled chestnuts into a pan with cold water to cover, bring to the boil, then simmer until barely tender. Drain. Dissolve the sugar (or use half sugar and half glucose) in the 600ml (1 pint) water and bring to the boil. Turn off heat, add chestnuts, cover and leave 24 hours. Remove lid, bring to simmering point and simmer 10 minutes. Turn off heat, cover and leave 24 hours. Add 10 drops

86

Candied fruits with fresh drinks and tisanes

of vanilla essence, bring to simmering point and simmer 10 minutes. Turn off heat, cover and leave 24 hours, then drain, put on to wire trays and leave until no longer sticky. By ensuring the syrup never really boils with the chestnuts in, they are likely to remain whole. However, if some do break up, mould the bits into balls about the size of chestnuts and dry.

Roll each in granulated sugar and wrap in a small piece of foil to prevent it becoming hard. Store in an airtight tin. Homemade marrons glacé should not be stored too long and it is wise to open one or two from time to time to check them.

Makes 1½kg (3lb)

Toffee Apples

Metric	Imperial
Small sweet dessert apples	Small sweet dessert apples
225g sugar	½lb sugar
150ml water	¼ pint water
50g butter	2oz butter
Pinch of cream of tartar	Pinch of cream of tartar
Few drops lemon juice	Few drops lemon juice

Wash and dry apples; remove remains of flowers and the stalks. Push a lollipop, or similar, stick into stalk ends. Put sugar and water into a small, strong, shallow pan, heat slowly and stir until the sugar has dissolved. Add butter and cream of tartar, bring to the boil and boil steadily. If possible, use a sugar thermometer and boil to 138°C/280°F; otherwise, watch carefully and remove from the heat when the syrup is toffee coloured (lightly-browned). Immediately add lemon juice to stop further browning. Quickly dip the apples one at a time into the syrup and turn to coat evenly. Lift out and drain, twisting the apple round and round until the drips stop, then stand on greaseproof paper until set. Use within 24 hours. When the syrup hardens too much to use or if any is left-over it can be diluted with 2 × 15ml spoons (2tbsps) water, stored and reboiled to 138°C/280°F as required.

Makes 4–6 apples

Frosted Grapes

These are used to decorate both savoury and sweet dishes such as baked ham or trifle, icecream dishes, etc.

Use seedless grapes, either white or black, and cut into small clusters. Brush with lightly beaten egg white and then dip into caster sugar to coat evenly. If possible, leave to dry overnight. Mint leaves can be frosted in the same way and used to decorate salads or summer drinks.

Real Lemonade or Orangeade

Metric	Imperial
4 large juicy lemons (or oranges)	4 large juicy lemons (or oranges)
1 litre water	2 pints water
225–450g sugar or honey	½–1lb sugar or honey

Wash the lemons well. Peel off rind, without white pith, put into a pan with the water and sugar and simmer for 20 minutes. Cool a little. Add the juice from the lemons and strain into a lidded container. Chill.

Some of the strips of rind can be used for decoration. If liked, add crushed mint leaves (or other herbs) for last 5 minutes of the simmering time.

Makes 1.5–1.8 litres (2½–3 pints)

Fresh Vegetable Cocktail

Metric	Imperial
2 inner stalks celery, with leaves, sliced	2 inner stalks celery, with leaves, sliced
1 medium carrot, peeled and sliced	1 medium carrot, peeled and sliced
5cm piece cucumber, peeled, seeded and sliced	2in piece cucumber, peeled, seeded and sliced
Small piece red or green pepper, sliced	Small piece red or green pepper, sliced
1 spring onion, sliced or small piece of onion	1 spring onion, sliced or small piece of onion
6 large stalks watercress	6 large stalks watercress
450ml tomato or orange juice, fresh or frozen	¾ pint tomato or orange juice, fresh or frozen
Mint or basil leaves or Worcestershire sauce	Mint or basil leaves or Worcestershire sauce
Salt and freshly ground black pepper	Salt and freshly ground black pepper
150ml water and ice cubes	¼ pint water and ice cubes

You need a blender for this recipe.

Put all the vegetables into the blender goblet with enough tomato or orange juice to cover the blades and blend ½ minute. Add mint leaves to orange juice; basil leaves or Worcestershire sauce to tomato juice. Add salt and pepper, the remaining juice and the water and ice cubes. Blend a further ½ minute.

If liked, pour through a fairly open sieve although the roughage in this drink is good for you. Serve as a starter or as a snack. Store in the refrigerator.

Makes 750ml (1¼ pints)

Icecream Soda

Metric	Imperial
225g fruit	½lb fruit
4 × 5ml spoons sugar	4tsps sugar
Approx. 350g vanilla icecream	Approx. 12oz vanilla icecream
Soda water, chilled	Soda water, chilled

Mash soft fruits such as strawberries and chop more firm fruit such as apricots, peaches and plums, with the sugar and mix until the sugar dissolves. Mix in 2 × 15ml spoons (2tbsps) of the icecream. Divide just over half the fruit between 4 tall glasses and put in the remaining icecream. Cover with remaining fruit and fill up with soda water. Serve with drinking straws and long spoons.

Serves 4

Tisanes

These are herbal infusions which are drunk either for their pleasant flavour or, by many people, for medicinal reasons. While commonly served as the first liquid of the day or as a bedtime drink, they are pleasant alternatives to morning coffee and afternoon tea.

Since their delicate flavours are adversely affected by metals, *never* use a metal teapot or metal strainer for tisanes.

Many herbs may be used: dried or fresh leaves of angelica, balm, basil, bergamot*, blackberry, borage, hyssop, lemon thyme, marjoram, all mints, parsley, raspberry, rosemary, sage or thyme.

Put 1 × 5ml spoon (1tsp) per person and 1 × 5ml spoon (1tsp) for the pot into a heated teapot if using dried herbs, or three times that quantity of fresh herbs (bruised to help extract their flavour). Pour on boiling water (milk can be used for bedtime drinks) and allow to infuse 5–10 minutes. Strain. Serve at once or chill, covered, in the refrigerator. Add honey and lemon juice to taste, if wished.

Dried or fresh flowers of camomile, elder and lime can be used in the same way for making teas.

Seeds of caraway and dill are also often used. Bruise them slightly to bring out the flavour, add to boiling water, simmer 5–10 minutes, strain and use. *Bergamot leaves should be simmered, in the same way, for 10 minutes.

Note It is important that the time given for infusing or simmering should not be exceeded or the brew will be bitter. For a stronger brew, increase the amount of herbs used.

Fresh Fruit Crushes
These are made in a blender. Oranges and lemons can be blended with water and sugar or with syrup, but fruits with less flavour need the addition of orange, apple, or other fruit juices. Soda water, tonic water, lemonade, etc. can also be added after blending.

Orange Crush

Metric	Imperial
4 oranges	4 oranges
½ lemon	½ lemon
2–4 × 15ml spoons sugar	2–4tbsps sugar
600ml iced water	1 pint iced water

Put the thinly peeled rind of 2 oranges, the sliced pulp (remove pips) and any juice from the pulp of all the oranges and the ½ lemon into the goblet. Add the sugar and half the water. Blend at high speed for half a minute. Add remaining water and blend 15 seconds. Strain and serve.
Serves 4

Strawberry Crush

Metric	Imperial
175g fresh or frozen strawberries	6oz fresh or frozen strawberries
1–2 × 5ml spoons sugar	1–2tsps sugar
300ml chilled orange juice	½ pint chilled orange juice
Ice cubes	Ice cubes

Put the strawberries into the blender goblet with the sugar and orange juice. Blend ½–1 minute until smooth. Serve with an ice cube in each glass. If preferred, blend strawberries and sugar, divide between the glasses and fill up with chilled soda water or lemonade.
Serves 4

Milk Shakes
These are made in the same way as Fruit Crushes, using fresh or frozen fruit or fruit purées. Use 175–225g (6–8oz) fruit to 600ml (1 pint) chilled milk and sweeten with sugar or sugar syrup if necessary. Use any type of milk including skimmed milk, skimmed milk powder reconstituted, diluted canned milk, etc.

Apricot Milk Shake

Metric	Imperial
225g apricot halves	8oz apricot halves
2 × 15ml spoons sugar syrup	2tbsps sugar syrup
600ml chilled milk	1 pint chilled milk

Put the apricots and syrup into blender goblet with half the milk. Blend until smooth, add remaining milk and blend until frothy.
Serves 4

Yogurt Drinks
The addition of 150ml (¼ pint) milk, or fruit or vegetable juice or purée to a 150g (5floz) carton of plain yogurt makes an excellent 'vitality' drink.

Cucumber and Mint Appetizer

Metric	Imperial
10cm piece cucumber, seeded and chopped	4in piece cucumber, seeded and chopped
1 × 15ml spoon roughly chopped mint leaves	1tbsp roughly chopped mint leaves
150ml chilled milk	¼ pint chilled milk
150ml plain yogurt	¼ pint plain yogurt
Salt and pepper	Salt and pepper

Put the cucumber and mint into the goblet with enough milk to cover the blades; blend about ½ minute at high speed. Add remaining ingredients, blend for a few seconds and serve.
Serves 2

Watercress Vitalizer

Metric	Imperial
¼ bunch watercress, washed	¼ bunch watercress, washed
Very small piece of onion	Very small piece of onion
150ml chilled milk	¼ pint chilled milk
150ml plain yogurt	¼ pint plain yogurt
Salt	Salt

Put the watercress and onion into the goblet with enough milk to cover the blades. Blend about ½ minute at high speed. Add remaining ingredients, blend for a few seconds and serve.
Note To chop very finely in a blender use only enough liquid to just cover the blades.
Serves 2

Mint Julep

Metric	Imperial
8–10 sprigs young mint	8–10 sprigs young mint
1 × 15ml spoon sugar	1tsp sugar
1 × 15ml spoon water	1tbsp water
Crushed ice	Crushed ice
Icing sugar, optional	Icing sugar, optional
Double measure of brandy, whisky, gin or bourbon	Double measure of brandy, whisky, gin or bourbon
Fresh fruit in season	Fresh fruit in season

Crush half the mint and the sugar with a spoon until the sugar dissolves. Add the water and mix until all the mint flavour is extracted. Take a tumbler or a large balloon wineglass, almost fill with crushed ice and push remaining mint in, stalks downwards. If liked, dip the leaves first in icing sugar. Strain the prepared mint mixture into the glass and pour in the spirit. Decorate the top of the ice with small pieces of fruit in season, choosing the most colourful available. Put in a couple of drinking straws and serve. If using brandy add just a dash of rum on top.
Serves 1

Index

The publishers would like to thank the following for their kind permission to reproduce the photographs in this book:

Roger Phillips 5; Rex Bamber 6–7, 11, 13, 15, 17, 19, 21, 23, 25, 27, 29, 31, 33, 35, 37, 39, 41, 43, 45, 47, 49, 51, 53, 55, 57, 59, 61, 63, 65, 67, 69, 71, 73, 75, 77, 79, 81, 83, 85, 87; Paul Kemp, endpapers.

Self Raising Flour.

Marg

Salt.   Dough Balls

Water.

Cook in oven

Self Raising Flour.

Marg